Jennifer Aldridge's

Archers'
Cookbook

Jennifer Aldridge's

Archers' Cookbook

Angela Piper

D&C
David and Charles

For my little sticky-fingered grandchildren Archie, Tilly, Charlie, Oscar and Alfie from Grangie with love.

A DAVID & CHARLES BOOK
Copyright © David & Charles Limited 2009

David & Charles is an F+W Media, Inc. company
4700 East Galbraith Road
Cincinnati, OH 45236

First published in the UK in 2009

Text copyright © Angela Piper 2009
Photographs copyright © see p. 176
Illustrations copyright © Sarah Bell 2009

ISBN-13: 978-0-7153-3338-9 hardback
ISBN-10: 0-7153-3338-0 hardback

Printed in the UK by Butler Tanner & Dennis
for David & Charles
Brunel House, Newton Abbot, Devon

Editorial & Design Director: Ali Myer
Commissioning Editor: Jane Trollope
Editorial Manager: Emily Pitcher
Editorial Assistant: James Brooks
Copy Editor: Susan Pitcher
Senior Design Advisor: Prudence Rogers
Art Editor: Sarah Clark
Production Controller: Alison Smith
Pre-press: Stuart Batley
Food Photographer: Mark Wood
Illustrator: Sarah Bell

www.davidandcharles.co.uk

David & Charles books are available from all good bookshops; alternatively you can contact our Orderline on 0870 9908222 or write to us at FREEPOST EX2 110, D&C Direct, Newton Abbot, TQ12 4ZZ (no stamp required UK only); US customers call 800-289-0963 and Canadian customers call 800-840-5220.

CONTENTS

INTRODUCTION

'Biscuits Ruairi, biscuits! Have you remembered your break-time biscuits?' Too late! Brian's big 4 x 4 swoops swiftly out of the yard at Home Farm on its way to the little local school at Loxley Barratt. Dressing-gowned and slippered, I start to clear away the crumby, mug-ridden muddle on the kitchen table, then drain the remaining grouts from the cafetière.

Oh how my life has changed! My husband Brian, that twilled and tweedy farmer, had promised me years of relaxed retirement. I had dreamed of waking each morning in a sun-drenched stone farmhouse, to the sighing sound of the breeze in the pine trees, sweet wild thyme scenting the air on an Andalucian hillside, and the distant Mediterranean a shimmering azure haze. But that is not to be.

My memories come flooding back to me. Brian, my wealthy, successful, land-owning husband, had been having an affair. Not a Mandy Beeseborough sort of fling, nor even a Caroline Bone-ish sort of besottedness; and certainly more than a muffled fumble in the airing cupboard with Betty Tucker. No, this was a monstrous and meaningful relationship with Siobhan Hathaway. Can you believe it? The doctor's wife of all people. I should have known – thinking back, the signs were pretty

obvious. All of Ambridge probably knew, with whispering in the village shop, murmurings along church pews and sniggering in the bus shelter. Of course there were the grovelling apologies, the flowers, the scent, the pleading for forgiveness. I had become quite used to this – but then came the heart-stopping hideous realisation that this time there was much, much more. Brian has a son. A precious son; the ultimate gift that I have never been able to give him. I really don't think he has ever forgiven me for that, because I have my own very special son, Adam, 'born out of wedlock', as they said some 40 years ago. Little Ruairi was a sad and lonely-looking child when I first saw him at his father's side – innocent, vulnerable and motherless after Siobhan had died. How could I possibly reject him? How could I not nurture and cherish Brian's young son and welcome him into our family fold?

A sudden rattle at the door handle brings me back to earth. A beaming Bert Fry stands in the kitchen doorway, his cloth cap crumpled in his hand and a muddy trug laden with vegetables at his feet. 'Come on, come in! Shut out this mad March wind. It's whipping round the yard and setting my kitchen curtains flapping.' There in the basket lie stalks of pale pink rhubarb and a mound of pearly new potatoes, each the size of a pigeon's egg. 'My Freda says to tell you she always pops some ginger in her rhubarb crumble and a snipping of fresh lovage on her buttery new potatoes'.

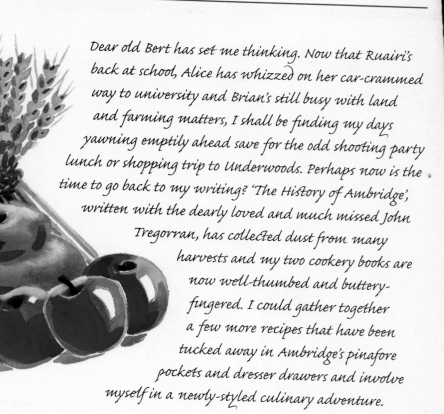

Dear old Bert has set me thinking. Now that Ruairi's back at school, Alice has whizzed on her car-crammed way to university and Brian's still busy with land and farming matters, I shall be finding my days yawning emptily ahead save for the odd shooting party lunch or shopping trip to Underwoods. Perhaps now is the time to go back to my writing? 'The History of Ambridge', written with the dearly loved and much missed John Tregorran, has collected dust from many harvests and my two cookery books are now well-thumbed and buttery-fingered. I could gather together a few more recipes that have been tucked away in Ambridge's pinafore pockets and dresser drawers and involve myself in a newly-styled culinary adventure.

And so, I would like you to picture the seasons in Ambridge with these recipes and capture the feel of the village through its enticing aromas and tempting treats. Be prepared to pick your way over the yard at Bridge Farm for some of Tony's muddy, crunchy, organic vegetables. Borrow a bicycle and Lynda will lead you to discover the tenderest green shoots for a springtime salad. Or just pack up a picnic and laze under the willows on the banks of the gently flowing Am. Adam always needs help in the heat of summer to pick

his luscious plump strawberries and Jill would be delighted if you knocked on the door of Glebe Cottage for a cosy chat and a pot of her sweet runny honey. Join Joe and he'll take you in Bartleby's trap, trotting down the lanes in search of the juiciest blackberries hidden in the bountiful Borsetshire hedgerows. But be sure to button up well when you join us for a jolly toffee-sucking, potato-munching evening at the November bonfire on the village green.

So pull on your wellies, pick up a basket and join me on a seasonal walk through the delightful Borsetshire village of Ambridge.

Jennifer.

SPRING

It's a blue-bright blustery morning. Woolly lambs gambol and nuzzle their mothers on Lakey Hill. Well-worn wintery undergarments wave merrily on the line at Keeper's Cottage, while worn-out Clarrie, bustling and breathless, attempts against all odds to waft away cobwebs and sweep kitchen dust into tidy piles. Grudgingly, curmudgeonly Joe is sent muttering into the yard away from his creaky old chair by the smoky stove.

Busy in The Bull's kitchen a slightly slimmer Freda speedily fashions Bert's pink and pot-forced rhubarb into a syrupy, crumbly pie.

Cottage windows are flung wide to catch the curtain-flapping breeze, doors swing and slam and wooden gates fly open to welcome in the fresh new feel to the countryside air.

Unleashed and released from the classroom confines, beaming little bodies with pigtails bouncing screech and squeal 'salt, pepper, vinegar, mustard', as the skipping ropes whip, twist, twizzle and entwine.

Along the willow-lined lane towards Ten Elms Rise Lynda Snell, puffing from pedalling is relieved to dismount from her sturdy steel steed to pluck, fresh from the verges, virgin green

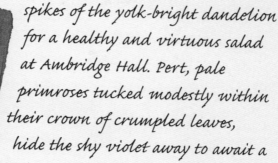

spikes of the yolk-bright dandelion for a healthy and virtuous salad at Ambridge Hall. Pert, pale primroses tucked modestly within their crown of crumpled leaves, hide the shy violet away to await a warming patch of midday sun to come teasing and reaching beneath the hawthorn's edge.

There's mid-morning madness in chilly St Stephen's. With duster-flicking keenness, a bevy of charitable god-fearing parishioners are Mansion-polishing the pews to a satin-smooth shine. Tapestry hassocks are fiercely pummelled, brasses huffed and wheezingly puffed on. All await Alan's beaming approval (maybe even a chipped mug of coffee and a custard cream if there's still time). Jars and vases are rinsed and filled and placed perilously on ledges, ready for Jill's armfuls of freshly picked yellow-frilled daffodils and twisted hazels' powdery-pollened catkins. 'Don't forget to put some on the Lawson-Hope shrine' shrills a well-meaning soul as she unties her apron strings.

In the deep yew shade in a corner of the churchyard, there's a dainty feathered fluttering as a bright-eyed blue tit pecks and pulls damp moss from a grey stone grave. Soon tiny speckled eggs will be cushioned in that soft mossy comfort. Nature's perfection, heralding a new life and a new year in the farming village of Ambridge.

MISTY MEMORIES

MARCH

Grange Farm's Grundy Boys

Young Edward Grundy, his worn woollen elbows leaning on a crumpled tablecloth, gulped down the last juicy mouthful of Clarrie's apple pie. No time to waste, he scraped back his chair across the lumpy linoed floor and raced out into the pot-holed yard. Chickens and kittens scattered as he and William skidded out through the leaning five-barred gate on their rattling, rusting bikes.

On sunlit days of early spring they saw snow-white blackthorn blossom and catkin-tasselled coppices, where the silence was broken only by chattering blackbirds or the joking laugh of a green woodpecker. Beneath their feet on the woodland floor wild windflowers, pale anemones, bowed their modest heads to the warming breeze. They tried to catch the early tawny tortoiseshells, flitting and fluttering on the bud-breaking hedgerows, and watched mad March hares sparring and chasing across brown, ploughed acres. They knew where to slip, slither and slide down celandine covered banks to collect long jewelled strings of toad spawn from deep damp ditches. Returning home only when tummies rumbled, they pedalled past young wild rabbits scuttling from their burrows as the pipistrelle skimmed low in the gathering twilight.

This was the true richness of the Ambridge countryside.

SIMNEL CAKE

The traditional Easter tea table isn't complete without Brookfield's Simnel Cake. My old Gran usually decorated it with eleven marzipan balls. However, this year speckled sugar eggs are in pride of place; more fun for the children, Jill thought.

FOR THE ALMOND PASTE
6oz (175g) caster sugar
6oz (175g) sifted icing sugar
12oz (350g) ground almonds
2 medium size eggs
1tsp lemon juice

FOR THE CAKE
6oz (175g) butter
6oz (175g) soft brown sugar
3 medium size eggs
grated zest of 1 lemon
grated zest of 1 orange
8oz (225g) plain flour
1tsp baking powder
¼tsp grated nutmeg
½tsp cinnamon
pinch of salt
1lb (450g) mixed dried fruit
2oz (55g) glacé cherries
1tbsp milk

To make the paste, combine the sugars with the ground almonds. Add the beaten egg and lemon juice. Work together well and roll out.

Grease and line a 7in (18cm) cake tin. Cream the butter and sugar, gradually adding the eggs and the grated lemon and orange zest. Sieve the flour and baking powder and add with the spices. Add the dried fruit, halved cherries and milk, and mix well.

Place half the mixture in the lined tin, smooth the top and cover with a round of almond paste. Add the remaining cake mixture and bake for 2¼–3 hours at 325°F/160°C/Gas 3.

When cold, cover the top of the cake with a round of almond paste. Decorate with sugared eggs or marzipan balls and tie a yellow ribbon round the cake.

Auntie Pru always said never bake more than one kind of cake in the oven at one time because they will both spoil.

EASTER BISCUITS

MAKES 24

These traditional Easter biscuits are always tied together in threes to represent the Trinity. Phoebe likes to help with a star shaped cutter, 'Like the stars in the sky that mummy can see too'.

5oz (140g) butter or margarine
5oz (140g) caster sugar
1 medium size egg
8oz (225g) plain flour
a pinch of cinnamon
2oz (55g) currants
1oz (25g) candied peel

Cream the butter and sugar and add the beaten egg. Stir in the sifted flour and cinnamon, currants and candied peel. Roll out ¼in (5mm) thick and cut out the biscuits with a fluted cutter. Cook on a baking tray for about 20 minutes at 400°F/200°C/Gas 6 until lightly coloured. Sprinkle with a little caster sugar.

HOT CROSS BUNS

MAKES 12

There was nothing quite like the warm cinnamony smell of Jill's hot cross buns baking in the Aga at Brookfield. A real Easter treat! Phil always thought they tasted especially good after church on Good Friday.

1lb (450g) plain flour
1tsp salt
1tsp ground cinnamon
1tsp mixed spice
2oz (55g) butter
2tbsp caster sugar
2oz (55g) currants
1oz (25g) candied peel
1oz (25g) fresh yeast
10fl oz (½pt/275ml) milk
1 medium size egg

Sieve the flour with the salt and spices into a large bowl. Rub in the butter and add the sugar (saving a little for the yeast), currants and candied peel.

Cream the yeast with the remaining sugar and add the tepid milk. Pour into the centre of the flour and leave to sponge for about 10 minutes, then mix to a dough with the beaten egg.

Cover the bowl with a clean tea towel and leave in a warm place to rise.

When the dough has doubled its size, turn on to a floured board, knead well and divide into twelve portions. Roll each into a flattened ball shape. Cut a deep cross on each one and place on a floured baking tray. Leave to prove for about 20 minutes, then bake in a hot oven at 400°/200°C/Gas 6 for about 20 minutes.

Brush the buns with a light glaze made by dissolving a little sugar in water.

MUESLI

Often bought in a packet these days but it makes Lynda feel very virtuous when she makes her own.

4tbsp porridge oats
approximately 10fl oz
  (½pt/300ml) water
3tbsp thick, whole milk yoghurt
1–2tbsp honey
juice of ½ lemon
3–4 dessert apples
1tbsp ground or chopped
  hazelnuts

Soak the oats overnight in almost 10fl oz (½pt/300ml) water. Next morning, stir in the yoghurt, honey and lemon juice. Grate the unpeeled apples and stir these in. Add the nuts, and serve.

KEDGEREE

Kedgeree makes a delicious breakfast alternative to bacon and eggs, or sausage and mushrooms. Always sprinkle on lots of freshly chopped parsley before serving.

8oz (225g) smoked haddock fillets
8oz (225g) rice
2oz (55g) butter
1 medium onion, chopped
2tsps mild curry powder
4 hard-boiled eggs
1tsp lemon juice
5fl oz (¼pt/150ml) single cream
1tsp chopped fresh parsley to
  garnish
salt and freshly ground black
  pepper

Cover the haddock fillets in cold water and poach for about 10 minutes, then drain, skin and flake the fish, discarding the bones.
  Simmer the rice in lightly salted water until soft but not soggy.
  Melt the butter in a large saucepan, add the onion and curry powder and cook over a low heat until transparent. Stir in the cooked rice, chopped hardboiled eggs, flaked fish, and lemon juice. Heat through, then add the cream, chopped parsley and adjust the seasoning.

SMOOTH AVOCADO SOUP

I believe Elizabeth persuaded Nelson to let her into the secrets of this recipe from his wine bar years ago.

1oz (25g) butter
1 medium onion, finely chopped
1lb (450g) sweet potatoes,
    peeled and diced
30fl oz (1½pt/850ml) chicken or
    vegetable stock
grated zest and juice of 1 orange
    and 1 lemon
2 ripe avocados
a dash of tabasco sauce
a pinch of mace, salt and pepper

Melt the butter in a large saucepan over a low heat and fry the onion and potatoes gently for 4 minutes. Add the stock and bring to the boil. Cover and simmer for 20 minutes. Then add the zest of the whole orange and that of half the lemon and the juice of both.

Halve the avocados, discard the stones and chop into pieces. Add to the soup mixture with the tabasco and seasoning. Purée the mixture in a blender or food processor.

Serve hot with croutons or cold with a whirl of single cream.

Jill says, 'Always remember to prick the shell of an egg to prevent it from bursting when being boiled.'

CARROT AND ORANGE SOUP

SERVES 6

The joy of this soup is that it can be served either hot with crusty rolls or croutons, or cold with swirls of cream or yoghurt and sprinkled with freshly snipped herbs on a balmy day.

1lb (450g) carrots
1 medium onion
2oz (55g) butter or
2tbsp vegetable oil
2tsp sugar
1tsp mace
salt and pepper
40fl oz (2pt/1.2l) chicken stock
  (or use a stock cube)
grated zest and juice of
  1 large orange
5fl oz (¼pt/150ml) natural yoghurt

Peel and chop the carrots and onion. Heat the butter in a large saucepan, add the carrot and onion and cook over a low heat for 10 minutes. Add the sugar, mace and seasoning and stir while adding the stock. Bring to the boil, then cover and simmer until tender.

Allow to cool a little, and then either push through a sieve or blend in a food processor until smooth. Stir in the orange zest and juice.

Pour the soup into individual bowls adding a swirl of yoghurt to serve.

ASPARAGUS AND HAM QUICHE

I must admit I think this is much more exciting made with fresh asparagus.

6oz (175g) shortcrust pastry
10oz (280g) can asparagus tips
4oz (115g) chopped ham
10fl oz (½pt/300ml) single cream
2 large size eggs
salt and black pepper

Line a 9in (23cm) fluted flan tin with the pastry. Prick the bottom lightly with a fork. Trim the asparagus into 1in (2.5cm) pieces and arrange in the base of the flan with the chopped ham.

Beat together the cream, eggs and seasoning and pour over the asparagus and ham.

Bake in a hot oven at 400°F/200°C/Gas 6 for 15 minutes, then reduce the heat to 350°F/180°C/Gas 4 and cook for a further 20 minutes, until the filling is set and golden brown.

Serve hot or cold.

GREEN SPINACH PIE WITH THREE CHEESES

SERVES 4–6

A hugely popular dish with Lynda's friends from the Borsetshire Wildlife Trust, perfectly green in every way! She serves it warm or cold, brightened with nasturtium flowers.

1 medium onion, finely chopped
2 cloves garlic, crushed
8oz (225g) white of leek, thinly sliced
2tbsp olive oil
1lb (450g) young spinach leaves
1oz (25g) fresh wholemeal
  breadcrumbs
2 medium size eggs
6oz (175g) Ricotta or curd cheese
6oz (175g) Gruyère cheese, grated
2oz (55g) parmesan, grated
salt and black pepper
10 sheets filo pastry
2oz (55g) unsalted butter, melted

Sweat the onion, garlic and leeks in a pan in the olive oil until soft.

Cook the spinach in a pan in very little water for 3–5 minutes. Drain well and press out any excess liquid. Allow to cool slightly. Stir in the breadcrumbs and the onion and leek mixture, together with the beaten eggs. Add the three cheeses and season well with salt and pepper.

Use half the filo pastry sheets to line an 8–9in (20–23cm) springform tin, brushing melted butter between each layer of pastry. Spoon the spinach and cheese filling into the pastry case, placing the remaining pastry sheets on top. Fold the edges of the lower sheets over the top sheets and brush the top with the remaining butter.

Bake at 375°F/190°C/Gas 5 for 25–30 minutes, or until the pie is golden-brown.

MISTY MEMORIES

APRIL

Ambridge

Light, feathery cirrus brushes plumes across a cerulean sky, while soulful willows, leaning over Lyttleton Brook, show a haze of misty green. The warming westerly races and chases down the slopes of Hassett Hill to whip the washing on the lines of Manorfield Close. Paisley-patterned pinafores and generously gusseted bloomers bounce amusingly into life. Gone are the days when Lettie Lawson-Hope up at The Manor marshalled her household troops to lift the dusty druggets from the Chinese rugs, pull off the dust sheets from the bergère suite and remove the balls of camphor from the dresser drawers. Gone too is the plunging of linen into Monday's tub of steaming soapy suds and the weary struggle with the heavy wooden mangle when young Doris Forrest, poking back her damp and straggling fringe under her stiff starched cotton cap, dreamed of evening walks down leafy country lanes and simple Sunday teas in her beamed and humble cottage home.

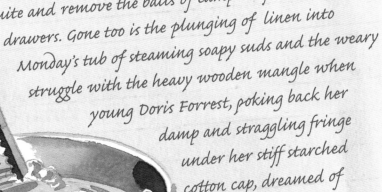

LILIAN'S POSH FISH PIE

'For ladies who lunch', says Lilian. 'So easy too. A fork in one hand and a glass in the other.' Although it's best as an aperitif, Lilian loves the bubbles of a Blanquette de Limoux to tickle her tongue as she enjoys this dish.

4 hard boiled eggs
3lb 5oz (1.5kg) of potatoes, peeled
4 garlic cloves, peeled
salt and freshly ground black pepper
3tbsp olive oil, or milk or cream
8oz (225g) peeled cooked prawns
1lb 1oz (500g) fresh spinach
4oz (115g) butter
ground nutmeg
¾lb (350g) monkfish, skinned, boned and cut into 2in (5cm) pieces
4tbsp crème fraîche or double cream
anchovy essence
handful of finely chopped fresh parsley

Hard boil the eggs, shell and cut into quarters. Boil the potatoes and garlic together until soft. Drain and mash with salt and olive oil or milk and leave to cool slightly.

Wash the spinach thoroughly and place in a saucepan – do not add water. Heat gently until it wilts, then raise the heat until it cooks (about 2–3 minutes). Drain and squeeze water out through a colander. Return to the pan adding black pepper, nutmeg and a knob of butter.

Spread the spinach on a well buttered large oven-proof dish. Put the monkfish into a shallow pan, cover with water. After about 5 minutes lift the fish from the pan and arrange the pieces on the spinach, scatter with the prawns and the quarters of hard boiled egg. Lightly whisk the crème fraîche or cream with a dash of anchovy essence and pour over the pie. Smooth the mashed potato over the top.

Place the dish on a baking sheet and cook in the oven 350°F/180°C/Gas 4 for 30 minutes.

Scatter with chopped parsley and serve.

SABRINA THWAITE'S SALMON STEAKS WITH A CREAMED LEEK SAUCE

Lithe and svelte, Sabrina seems not to gain an ounce, so this must be a healthy recipe.

4 salmon steaks (or fillets)
4 sprigs of chervil or tarragon
3tbsp white wine
salt and freshly ground black pepper

FOR THE SAUCE
1oz (25g) butter
6oz (175g) white or pale green
 leeks, chopped
1 small shallot, finely chopped
½pt (300ml) vegetable stock or
 bouillon
3tbsp crème fraîche
salt and freshly ground black pepper
good squeeze of lemon
handful of chopped fresh tarragon

Melt the butter, add the leeks and shallot, and cook slowly until soft, but not brown. Add the stock and crème fraîche and simmer for 10 minutes. Liquidize and adjust the seasoning to taste, before adding the chopped tarragon and a good squeeze of lemon.

Place the salmon steaks on a large sheet of foil and pour the white wine on each steak. Season with salt and pepper and put the sprig of chervil or tarragon on top of each one. Fold the foil over the top to make a loose parcel.

Place in the preheated oven 350°F/180°C/Gas 4) for 10–15 minutes.

Remove the herbs and transfer each steak to a warmed serving dish and pour over the sauce. Decorate with a sprig of watercress or parsley.

KATE'S BOBOTIE

SERVES 4

A savoury dish made with minced beef and almonds. Lucas cooked this when I went to see Kate, Nolly and baby Sipho in Johannesburg.

2 large onions, chopped
1tbsp cooking oil
1lb (450g) minced beef
1tbsp curry powder
1 slice bread, brown or white
   (crusts removed)
10fl oz (½pt/300ml) milk
1tbsp chopped almonds
juice of 1 lemon
1tsp dried mixed herbs
10fl oz (½pt/300ml) stock
salt and pepper
2 medium size eggs

Fry the chopped onion in the oil until transparent, then add the meat, stirring frequently until browned. Add the curry powder. Soak the bread in a little of the milk, mash it with a fork and mix into the meat and onion. Add the almonds, lemon juice, herbs, stock and seasoning. Cook the mixture slowly for a few minutes, then turn into an oven-proof dish. Beat the eggs with the remaining milk and pour over the beef.

Cook in a slow to moderate oven at 325°F/160°C/Gas 3 for about an hour, until the top is brown and bubbling.

Sender's name and address
JENNIFER ALDRIDGE
HOME FARM
AMBRIDGE
Postcode NR BORCHESTER

TARTE AU CITRON (AU JEAN-PAUL)

This is a slightly simplified version from the erstwhile chef. Do use un-waxed fruit and, if you prefer the tart sharper to the taste buds, use more lemon zest.

4oz (115g) butter
6oz (175g) plain flour
1oz (25g) icing sugar
1tbsp water

FOR THE FILLING
4oz (115g) caster sugar
3 medium size eggs, separated
grated zest and juice of 1 orange
 and 1 large lemon
5fl oz (150ml/¼pt) double cream
1oz (25g) icing sugar

In a saucepan melt the butter over a low heat and sieve in the flour and icing sugar, add the water and mix to a soft dough.

Press into an 8in (20cm) flan tin or dish, prick the base with a fork and bake blind for 15 minutes at 350°F/180°C/Gas 4.

To make the filling, put the caster sugar, egg yolks and grated zest in a bowl. Whisk thoroughly. Beat in the cream and juice until blended. Beat the egg whites until stiff and carefully fold into the mixture. Pour into the cooked pastry case.

Lower the oven temperature to 300°F/150°C/Gas 2 and cook until golden brown and set.

Sieve icing sugar over the tart before serving with whipped cream, fromage frais or yoghurt.

FRUITY FLORENTINES

With these in the oven the kitchen smells deliciously of a French patisserie.

4oz (115g) butter or margarine
4oz (115g) caster sugar
2tbsp clear honey
2tbsp mixed peel, chopped
2tbsp glace cherries, chopped
1tbsp sultanas
1tbsp blanched almonds, chopped
4oz (115g) plain flour
4oz (115g) plain chocolate

Line baking sheets with non-stick parchment.

Melt the butter in a saucepan, stir in the sugar and honey and bring slowly to the boil while stirring. Remove from the heat and add the mixed peel, cherries, sultanas, almonds and flour. Stir thoroughly and allow to cool slightly.

Drop heaped teaspoons of the mixture on to the baking sheets, allowing space to spread, and bake for 10–12 minutes at 350°F/180C/Gas 4 until golden brown.

Allow to cool for 1–2 minutes before removing with a palette knife. Place on a wire tray to cool further.

Melt the chocolate in a basin over a pan of boiling water, then spoon and spread the chocolate over the smooth surface of each biscuit, making swirled patterns with a fork.

LEMON-ICED SHORTBREAD

These are very popular in the Lower Loxley Orangery. Tangy and decidedly moreish, the ground rice gives the biscuits an interesting texture.

4oz (115g) butter
2oz (55g) caster sugar
grated zest of half a lemon
4oz (115g) plain flour
2oz (55g) ground rice

FOR THE LEMON ICING
1tbsp hot water
1tbsp lemon juice
4oz (115g) icing sugar, sieved

Cream the butter and the sugar together until soft. Beat in the grated lemon zest. Stir in the flour and ground rice and mix to a smooth dough.

Roll the dough out thinly and cut out rounds with a fluted biscuit cutter. Place the rounds on greased baking sheets and prick the surface with a fork. Bake in the oven at 350°F/180°C/Gas 4 for 15 minutes, or until golden.

To make the icing, add the water and lemon juice to the icing sugar and mix until smooth. When the biscuits are cool, spread on the icing.

APRICOT YOGHURT SCONES

'You spoil me, Pat', says Tony in a crumbly sort of mumble. He loves them warm and spread with butter.

8oz (225g) self-raising flour (half white,
  half wholewheat)
pinch of salt
1oz (25g) caster sugar
2oz (55g) lard
2oz (55g) chopped dried apricots
  (ready-soaked)
6fl oz (175ml) apricot yoghurt

Sift the flour, salt and sugar together. Rub in the lard and then add the chopped apricots. Mix in the yoghurt to form a soft dough, adding a little milk if the mixture is too stiff.
  Roll the mixture out on a floured board and cut into rounds with a pastry cutter. Brush with milk and place on a greased baking tray, and bake in a hot oven at 425°F/220°C/Gas 7 for about 10 minutes or until golden-brown.

ROSIE'S ROCK BUNS

MAKES ABOUT 12

Clarrie's sister Rosie suggested this simple recipe. They're a bit plain for little George's liking.

8oz (225g) plain flour
½tsp salt
2tsp baking powder
2oz (55g) margarine or butter
1oz (25g) lard
3oz (85g) brown sugar
2oz (55g) currants
2oz (55g) candied peel
½tsp cinnamon
1 medium size egg
a little milk
a little extra sugar and cinnamon

Sift the flour, salt and baking powder into a bowl. Rub in the butter and fat. When it resembles fine breadcrumbs add the sugar, currants, peel and cinnamon.
  Beat the egg with a little milk, make a well in the centre of the dry ingredients and pour this in, mixing thoroughly.
  Place the mixture into little rounds on a greased baking tray and sprinkle the tops with the extra sugar and cinnamon. Bake for about 15 minutes at 450°F/230°C/Gas 8.

MISTY MEMORIES

May

Whitsuntide Treat

One gleaming morning at the end of
May, when pink blossoms were still
frothy on orchard branches and
cowslips clustered in the dew-damp
grass, a chattering gaggle of Ambridge's
pensioners were bunched at the bus-stop on the village green.
Cloth caps were set at jaunty angles, brogues brown-polished to a conker-like
gleam. Jethro puffed on a Woodbine as the tension mounted. Martha sucked on
a humbug with the journey in mind. Then right on time, round the bend by the
duck pond, came the old bus with a rattle and a whine. Up they all clambered,
wheezing and eager, jostling for seats by the window or the aisle. 'Everyone
here?', said the Wharton's driver, 'then off we go', on the well-earned, long
yearned for Whitsuntide day trip: the sun and fun, tea and a bun, annual
outing to the wide, grey watery waste of Weston-upon-the-Sea.

SALMON AND WATERCRESS PARCELS WITH SORREL SAUCE

If it's difficult to find sorrel use some small spinach leaves instead. Perfect picnic parcels as well; without the sauce of course!

4 medium pieces of salmon fillet, approx 6oz (175g) each
1 small bunch watercress
2oz (55g) melted butter
grated zest of half a lemon
pinch of salt
freshly ground black pepper
1 pkt (400g) filo pastry (8 sheets – square ones are best. Trim large sheets as necessary to make neat parcels)
4tbsp soured cream

FOR THE SAUCE

4 spring onions, finely chopped
4fl oz (125ml) dry white wine
5fl oz (150ml) thick double cream
4oz (115g) sorrel or small spinach leaves, finely shredded
a few sprigs of parsley and tarragon

Remove carefully any fine bones and skin from the salmon.

Rinse the watercress, discarding any tough stems, and dry on kitchen paper. Chop finely.

Mix the lemon zest and salt and pepper into the cream.

Brush 4 sheets of filo with melted butter, top each with a second sheet and brush again. Place a piece of salmon fillet on each. Scatter the watercress on the salmon and top with a tablespoon of the seasoned sour cream. Gather the pastry up around the fish to make parcels, and place on a baking sheet. Brush the parcels with the remaining melted butter.

Bake in a preheated oven at 375°F/190°C/Gas 5 for about 20 minutes, or until the pastry is crisp and golden.

To make the sauce, cook the chopped spring onions gently in the white wine until the wine is reduced by half. Add the cream and heat gently until boiling and slightly thickened. Add the shredded sorrel leaves and chopped parsley and tarragon. Season with salt and white or lemon pepper.

Blend to a purée in a liquidiser or food processor. Reheat and keep the sauce warm until required.

MY SIMPLE PASTA WITH TUNA, GARLIC AND SUN-DRIED TOMATOES

SERVES 2–3

It takes only a few minutes to prepare and make this simple savoury pasta. I must suggest it to Alice when she next comes home.

4tbsp olive oil
1 small onion, chopped
2 garlic cloves, chopped
6 dried tomato halves, sliced
salt and pepper
7oz (200g) can tuna, drained and flaked
2tsp fresh oregano or parsley
8oz (225g) dried pasta, macaroni
  or penne

Heat the oil in a saucepan and fry the onion until it softens, then add the garlic. Stir in the tomatoes, salt and pepper and cook for 5 minutes over a low heat. Add the tuna fish and oregano or parsley and heat through for 2 minutes.

Cook the pasta in boiling salted water for the required length of time, then drain and place in a warmed serving dish.

Pour the sauce over the pasta. This can be served with a sprinkling of grated parmesan cheese on top if desired.

NOTES

Darling Alice,
Do pop home again to see us before too long.
I know that Spearmint is missing you.
Lots of love from us all xx

PIP'S QUICK-FIX SPICY STIR-FRY

SERVES 2

While Ruth's busy doing the milking, Pip can quickly rustle up a supper before leaping off for an evening at the Young Farmers' Club.

Choose a random selection of vegetables (to include broccoli, peas, baby corn and finely sliced carrot)
a handful of mushrooms
2 spring onions
1 clove garlic
small knob of ginger, peeled and chopped
2tbsp olive or groundnut oil
salt and pepper

Chop the mushrooms and broccoli into bite-size pieces, slice the spring onions into 1in (2.5cm) sticks and crush the garlic to release all of the flavour.

Heat the oil in a frying pan or wok until it shimmers, then toss in spring onions, garlic and ginger. Fry for about 1 minute, taking care that the garlic doesn't singe, then add the remaining vegetables. Move the food around the pan with a spatula or Chinese scoop so that it all sizzles. It will be crisp, but tender in about 2 or 3 minutes.

Season to taste and serve on rice.

UNCLE WALTER'S WISDOM:
'Be out in the fields
when the sun shines bright
And keep all yer sleep
for the dark hours of night.'

CREAMY CURRIED CHICKEN WITH LEMON RICE

This is Shula's delicious recipe. I wonder if she used to make this for Mark?

1lb (500g) cooked chicken, cut into 1in
  (2.5cm) pieces
2tbsp nut oil
2 medium onions, peeled and chopped
2 sticks celery, chopped
6 slices root ginger, finely chopped
1 green pepper, deseeded chopped
1 green chilli, very finely chopped
1tbsp plain flour
1tbsp garam masala
1tsp ground turmeric
3 cloves garlic, crushed
1pt (600ml) chicken stock or bouillon
4tbsp crème fraîche
salt and pepper

Heat the oil in a flame proof casserole. Soften the onion, celery, ginger, green pepper and chilli.
Add the chicken and combine with these ingredients.
Stir in the flour, spices and garlic, then carefully add the stock. Cover the pan and simmer for 20 minutes.
Stir in the crème fraîche and season, then return to gentle heat for 15 minutes.

FOR THE LEMON RICE

2 shallots, peeled and chopped
2tbsp butter
8oz (225g) Basmati rice
grated zest and juice of 1 large lemon
salt and pepper
1pt (600ml) water

Fry the shallots in butter until soft and transparent. Stir in the rice, lemon zest and juice.
Season with salt and pepper.
Add the water and half cover the pan, and simmer until the rice is tender and the water absorbed.

SEARED TUNA WITH LIME BUTTER AND CAPERS

SERVES 4

When the Beeseboroughs popped round for supper, I rustled this up with virtually no effort at all. Brian left all his capers...and so did Mandy. I wonder why?

4 medium-sized tuna steaks
1tbsp olive oil
2oz (55g) butter
1tbsp capers
2 unwaxed limes
salt and pepper

Heat a ridged steak pan over a high heat and put in half the oil and butter. Place the tuna steaks on the pan so they sear on the ridges. Leave to cook for about 2 minutes, depending on the thickness of the steaks. Turn and cook on the other side. Transfer to a warmed serving dish.

Squeeze the juice together with 1tbsp of grated zest from the limes into the fats in the pan, adding the capers and remaining butter. When bubbling and slightly reduced, pour the sauce over the steaks. Serve immediately and season to taste.

HOME FARM'S MOROCCAN LAMB TAGINE

I cook this hours in advance, leaving me plenty of time to meet Ruairi from school and pop in to see Mum for a cosy cuppa. The longer it's left, the more delicious it becomes. 'Oh darling, I can almost feel the warmth of the sun and smell the spices in the souk', gushes Brian.

2 lamb shanks (or one each if your guests have healthy appetites!)
1 medium size onion, chopped
4 cloves of garlic, peeled and roughly chopped
2in (5cm) piece of root ginger, peeled and chopped
2 heaped tsp cinnamon
2 heaped tsp coriander, ground
2 heaped tsp cumin
2tbsp olive oil
a good handful of dried apricots (ready-soaked)
juice and zest of 1 orange
2oz (55g) skinned almonds
2 medium size sweet potatoes, peeled and chopped into chunks
1tsp honey
salt and pepper
2pt (1.2l) water

In a large heavy saucepan or tagine lightly fry the onion and garlic. When golden add the ginger, spices and apricots, and the lamb shanks. Turn the lamb until golden, then add the orange zest and juice. Add the almonds and sweet potatoes and stir in the honey.

Now cover with water and leave on a low heat or in the oven on a low temperature for about 1½ hours.

Remove the meat from the bone (it should be mouth-watering tender and fall away easily) and serve with my herb and citrus couscous overleaf.

HERB AND CITRUS COUSCOUS

Put **20fl oz (1pt/400ml) boiling water**
  into a bowl.
Add **7oz (200g) couscous**
1tbsp olive oil
Cover the bowl and leave for 10 minutes.

Add a knob of butter and fluff up with a fork,
before adding grated zest and juice of an
orange, a handful of chopped mint and 1tbsp
of white wine vinegar.

OR
Add grated zest and juice of a lemon,
a handful of chopped coriander leaves and
1tbsp of white wine vinegar.
  Combine all the ingredients and season
with salt and pepper to taste.
  Serve warm, or cold the next day
with salad.

38
Spring

LILIAN'S RICH TIRAMISU

Still popular with coffee addicts, although Lilian's always rather too generous with the brandy.

10fl oz (½pt/300ml) strong
   black coffee
2tbsp coffee liqueur or brandy
24 boudoir sponge finger biscuits
3 medium size eggs, separated
3tbsp caster sugar
2 x 9oz (250g) cartons
   mascarpone cheese
a little cocoa powder

Mix the coffee and liqueur together. Immerse the sponge fingers in the mixture one at a time, then line the bottom of a glass trifle bowl with half of them.

Whisk or beat the egg yolks with the sugar until pale and thick. Add the mascarpone gradually until the mixture is evenly blended.

Whisk the egg whites until they stand in stiff peaks then fold into the mascarpone mixture.

Spread half the mixture over the sponge fingers in the trifle bowl, then add another layer of coffee-soaked sponge fingers and spread the remaining mascarpone on top.

Decorate liberally with sifted cocoa powder and chill overnight, or for at least 6 hours. Serve chilled.

GRANNY PERKINS' LEMON PUDDING

SERVES 4–6

Nobody ever makes this as well as Granny Perkins did. The top of her pudding was always crisp and golden, while underneath was a smooth and lemony sauce.

3oz (85g) butter or margarine
4oz (115g) caster sugar
juice and zest of 2 small lemons
2oz (55g) plain flour
½tsp baking powder
2 medium eggs, separated
5fl oz (¼pt/150ml) milk

Cream the butter and sugar with the grated lemon zest until light and fluffy. Fold in the sifted flour and baking powder. Add the egg yolks only and whisk together with the lemon juice and milk.

Beat the egg whites stiffly until standing in peaks and fold into the lemon mixture.

Bake in a buttered 6in (15cm) soufflé dish placed within a baking tin half-filled with water, for 40 minutes at 350°F/180°C/Gas 4.

Serve immediately, preferably with whipped cream.

Betty Tucker said she made her fruit cakes moist by adding a tablespoon of marmalade in preference to chopped candied peel.

PADDINGTON'S CHOCOLATE AND ORANGE PUDDING

SERVES 4–6

At Home Farm we use rich chocolate spread on alternate slices of brioche, instead of melted plain chocolate. This really is one of Ruairi's favourites.

7oz (200g) plain chocolate, broken into pieces
2oz (55g) unsalted butter
8oz (225g) sliced brioche loaf
4tbsp marmalade
3 eggs
1oz (25g) caster sugar
20fl oz (1pt/600ml) full cream milk

Grease a 3pt (1.8 l) oven-proof dish. Melt together the chocolate and half the butter in a basin over a pan of simmering water.

Spread the slices of brioche with marmalade and place one layer in the dish, before putting over spoonfuls of the chocolate sauce. Place another layer of brioche and sauce on top, and continue until there is none of either left. Melt the rest of the butter and whisk together with the eggs, sugar and milk. Pour over the brioche and leave to soak for 10 minutes.

Bake in a preheated oven at 50°F/180°C/Gas 4) for about 45 minutes until set.

FREDA'S RHUBARB AND GINGER CRUMBLE

SERVES 4

*Bert's very proud of his delicate, pale pink, early rhubarb.
Freda turns it into a good old-fashioned crumble.*

2oz (55g) hard margarine or butter
4oz (115g) plain flour
2oz (55g) soft brown sugar
1tsp ground ginger
1lb (450g) rhubarb
1tbsp chopped preserved ginger
2tbsp ginger syrup
5oz (140g) caster sugar

Put the margarine into a bowl and rub into the flour until it resembles fine breadcrumbs. Stir in the soft brown sugar and ground ginger.

Peel the rhubarb sticks (unless they are very young and tender) and cut into ½in (1cm) pieces. Place these with the chopped preserved ginger and syrup and the caster sugar in a 2pt (1.2l) pie dish. Cover the fruit with the crumble mixture, pressing it down gently.

Bake in the oven at 350°F/180°C/Gas 4 for about 40 minutes until crisp and golden.

CREAMY APRICOT FLAN

SERVES 8

This is deliciously rich, especially when drizzled with chocolate sauce.
It always reminds me of the stylish charm of Nelson's wine bar.

5fl oz (¼pt/150ml) double cream
4oz (115g) caster sugar
2tbsp brandy
6oz (175g) full fat cream cheese
grated zest of 1 orange
8oz (225g) dried apricots
 (ready-soaked), chopped

FOR THE CRUST
12oz (350g) chocolate chip biscuits
3oz (75g) butter, melted
2oz (50g) good quality plain chocolate,
 plus extra to decorate
2oz (50g) toasted almonds, chopped

To make the crust, put the biscuits in a large plastic bag and crush them to crumbs with a rolling pin or crush them in a food processor.

Melt the butter and chocolate in a bowl set over a pan of simmering water, making sure the water is not touching the base of the bowl. Remove from the heat and stir in the biscuit crumbs and chopped almonds.

Press the mixture as firmly as possible over the base and up the sides of a 23cm (9in) springform cake tin. Put this in the refrigerator for 30 minutes or so to harden.

Whip the cream with the sugar and brandy and beat in the cream cheese and orange zest. Fold in the chopped apricots and fill the flan case.

Decorate with grated chocolate and chill before serving.

Chocolate fudge cake.

rgarine (175g)
room temperature)
ar (175g)
2oz gr almonds (50g)
6oz plain flour (175g)
sieved with 2½ oz
cocoa (65g)
1½ teaspoon Bread
blended
milk

SUMMER

Oh how I love the length of summer days! Under cream canvas I lie, shaded by an extravagant stretch of a colonial-styled sun umbrella, comfortably cushioned on a slatted teak steamer. Listless too, Lilian dabbles her perfectly pedicured toes in the cool, clear water of our glistening, limpid pool. A glass of chilled Chardonnay and a curled sliver or two of smoked salmon sit on a table beside her. Bliss. Serene, stupefying, summery bliss. A gentle breeze flutters and flaps and lightly lifts the glossy pages of 'Borsetshire Life'. Then I hear the humming and the buzzing of a pollen-powdered bumble bee as it nuzzles deep into the trumpet of a fading, freckled foxglove.

A distant droning tells the tale of dusty harvesting. Brian, with shirt sleeves rolled, sitting high as the sky in our combine's five-star air-conditioned luxury, surveys the glorious, golden scene. Hedges and ditches have been stealthily, wealthily, cruelly plundered. Their berried seed-rich cover stolen. Now, this greedy beast gorges and gobbles its giant way across vast acres of winter-sown wheat. But only too soon this seasonal, busy burst of expansive energy leads to winter's frugality when this monstrous machine is lengthily, idly and expensively stored. In Jethro's day sweet-scented sheaves were stacked in stooks. Workers, as brown and wrinkled as pickled walnuts, wielded pitchforks from shimmering dawn till bat-skimming dusk; just snatching a brief rest and bite of a crusty cob with a lump of cheese, if they were lucky, right there on the poppy-peppered edge of the cornfield.

Lynda serves iced tea combined with ginger ale for a refreshing summer drink. She pours the tea over ice, adds sugar and tops with ginger ale. Add a squeeze of lemon or lime juice to taste.

A favourite summer song drifts through my head…'…the corn is as high as an elephant's eye…O-o-o-klahoma…'; when suddenly the daydream is broken by reality. 'O-o-o…Oh help, Lilian! I've just remembered! I'm on ticket-money-taking duty at Adam's maize-maze this afternoon. Be a darling, do. Pop your feet back into those gold strappy sandals and lend me a hand. I can't be late. It's Ambridge v Edgeley and there are scones to be buttered before the batting's all over and iced sponge to be sliced for Shula's cricket match tea. And then, horror of horrors, Brian's accepted an invite to the ghastly Beeseboroughs for a frightful fork supper. Oh, what a beastly bore!'

MISTY MEMORIES

JUNE

The Brownies' Summer Picnic

Lakey Hill, brown and ridged on one side, speckled with heather and studded with gorse on the other. It's not particularly dramatic but the gently rising slopes hold so many secrets. Up that sandy path villagers have trod for centuries, the wind whistling in their ears and stinging their eyes on winter afternoons. They have felt the heady warmth of summer days, the soothing drone of bees softening their brows.

On a bright morning in June, as the spring brilliance of hedges turned a gentler shade of green and yellow-hammers darted, you'd see a crocodile of little legs, keen with youth's fresh anticipation of a sun-filled, fun-filled day. Bouncing bags knocking against knees, plastic carriers proclaiming 'Underwoods – The Best in Borchester', the Ambridge Brownie pack moved towards Lakey Hill. Last to climb the wooden stile were chided. 'Buck up, Becky, we haven't got all day.'

But they had. A day that unfurled with simple, wholesome, tumbling fun. 'Run and find some "eggs and bacon", buttercups and "granny's bonnets"', Brown Owl hooted. 'First back to the Toadstool earns five points. Well done Emma! Five for the Finches'. Later, as the damp shadows stretched across the eastern side of the hill, those weary little plimsolled feet plodded down the path to meet the ribbon of lane that wound towards home.

FILO PASTRY PARCELS

Perfect little parcels for any picnic, although they'll probably cover the rug with crumbs.

3 shallots
3oz (85g) butter
10oz (280g) can asparagus spears,
  drained and chopped
2tbsp plain flour
10fl oz (½pt/300ml) milk
4oz (115g) Gruyère cheese, grated
salt and freshly ground black pepper
14oz (400g) filo pastry

Slice the shallots and soften in 1oz (25g) of melted butter and cook gently for 2–3 minutes. Add the asparagus (having discarded any woody stems) and heat through. Add the flour, heat gently and then stir in the milk to make a smooth sauce. Add the grated Gruyère and season with salt and black pepper.

Melt the remaining 2oz (55g) butter in a pan. Spread out the filo pastry sheets on a clean worktop and brush the butter on them, one at a time.
(Filo pastry dries out very quickly so keep it covered with a damp tea towel.)
  Cut the pastry into 5 in (13cm) squares, lay three squares on top of each other, and spoon a large teaspoonful of the asparagus mixture on to the centre of each square. Gather up the corners and pinch them together to form a sealed parcel. Brush the outside of each parcel with melted butter.
  Place them on a buttered baking tray and bake at 375°F/190°C/Gas 5 for 10–15 minutes, until crisp and golden. Freeze any unused filo pastry.

SESAME SCOTCH EGGS

MAKES 2

Phoebe helps to squash the sausage meat around the eggs. If the sesame seeds won't stick, roll the Scotch eggs in beaten egg rather than milk.

2 medium size eggs
4oz (115g) sausage meat
2tbsp sesame seeds
a little milk
a little flour

Put the eggs into a pan of cold water, bring to the boil, and boil for 10 minutes. Cool in a bowl of cold water and then remove the shells.

Divide the sausage meat into two halves and roll out each piece on a floured board.

Place one egg in the centre of each piece of sausage meat and wrap the sausage meat around it, making sure that all the joins are pinched together. Now roll each Scotch egg, first in milk and then in sesame seeds, making sure that the sesame seeds are pressed firmly into the meat.

Wrap each one in foil and bake in the oven at 375°F/190°/Gas 5 for 45-50 minutes.

Allow to cool and then pack in fresh foil for the picnic.

Cure the tingling of nettle stings by rubbing with rosemary, sage, mint or the well-known dock leaves.

STRAWBERRY CREAM CROISSANTS

Adam has introduced these to Ruairi. We have such a glut of strawberries. Take plenty of paper napkins or kitchen roll to mop up the oozing cream on chins and T-shirts.

4 croissants
2fl oz (50ml) double cream
2oz (55g) fromage frais
1tbsp icing sugar
2tbsp redcurrant jelly (or raspberry jam)
6oz (170g) ripe strawberries

Slice the croissants horizontally but do not cut right through.

Whip the double cream, adding the fromage frais and the icing sugar.

Open the croissants and spread the jelly on the inside. Spoon in the cream, spreading it as evenly as possible, finally filling with sliced strawberries. Wrap each croissant in foil and chill in a refrigerator.

Transport to the picnic in a cool box if possible.

CHOCOLATE CRUNCHIES

MAKES ABOUT 36 BISCUITS

These will keep crisp for a long time in a tin or plastic box.

8oz (225g) butter or hard margarine
4oz (115g) caster sugar
1tsp vanilla essence
8oz (225g) self-raising flour
1oz (25g) cocoa
1oz (25g) drinking chocolate

Cream together the butter and sugar with the vanilla essence until pale and fluffy.

Gradually beat in the sifted flour, cocoa and drinking chocolate.

With rinsed hands roll the mixture into spheres the size of golf balls. Then place on ungreased baking trays and flatten with a damp fork.

Bake in a moderate oven at 350°F/180°C/Gas 4 for 8–10 minutes. Transfer to a wire rack to cool.

LITTLE GEORGE'S STICKY FINGERS

MAKES 10–12 FINGERS

FOR THE SHORTBREAD BASE

4oz (115g) butter or margarine

2oz (55g) caster sugar

4oz (115g) self-raising flour

1½tsp vanilla essence

FOR THE TOFFEE TOPPING

4oz (115g) soft brown sugar

4oz (115g) butter or margarine

2tbsp golden syrup

1 small tin condensed milk

6oz (170g) dark chocolate

Cream the butter and sugar together and add the vanilla essence and flour. Mix to a smooth paste and spread into a Swiss roll tin.

Bake in the oven at 350°F/180°C/Gas 4 for 20 minutes or until golden.

Now make the toffee topping. Melt the sugar, butter, syrup and condensed milk together in a saucepan over a moderate heat until the mixture is thick enough to leave the side of the pan. Bring to the boil, stirring all the time, and boil for 4 minutes. Pour over the shortbread and leave to cool. Melt 6oz (170g) chocolate and pour over the toffee. Cut into fingers when cold.

HOME-MADE LEMON DRINK

Thirst-quenching, healthy and wholesome. Do you think they made this for the stook-stacking farm workers in years gone by?

6 lemons
2lb (900g) granulated sugar
40fl oz (1.2l/2pt) water, boiling

Scrub the lemons and peel thinly with a sharp knife. Squeeze the juice from them and place in a jug with the sugar and lemon zest. Cover and stand in a cool place for an hour.

Slowly pour over the boiling water and allow to stand over-night. Strain into bottles. Keep in a cool place. Dilute to taste before serving.

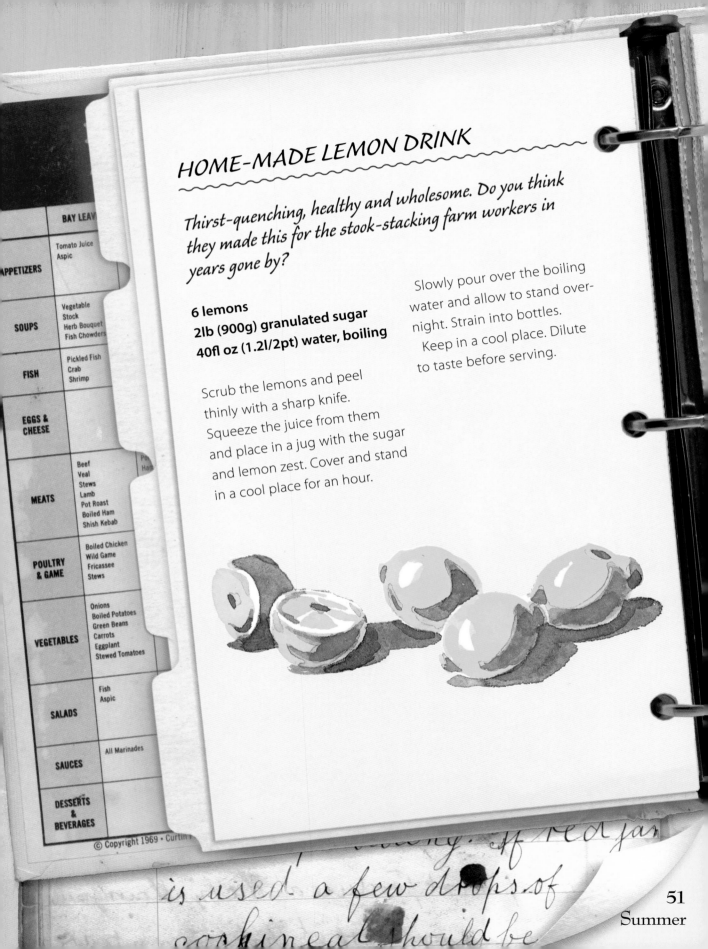

BAY LEAV

APPETIZERS | Tomato Juice / Aspic

SOUPS | Vegetable Stock / Herb Bouquet / Fish Chowders

FISH | Pickled Fish / Crab / Shrimp

EGGS & CHEESE

MEATS | Beef / Veal / Stews / Lamb / Pot Roast / Boiled Ham / Shish Kebab

POULTRY & GAME | Boiled Chicken / Wild Game / Fricassee / Stews

VEGETABLES | Onions / Boiled Potatoes / Green Beans / Carrots / Eggplant / Stewed Tomatoes

SALADS | Fish / Aspic

SAUCES | All Marinades

DESSERTS & BEVERAGES

© Copyright 1969 • Curtin

MISTY MEMORIES

JULY

St Stephen's Summer Fete

It was the post-shearing, pre-harvesting, most suitable Saturday in July, dawning fresh and breezily bright. Multi-coloured flags and bunting fluttered over the stalls on the village green. Gold-braided, brass-buttoned George Barford, his collar too tight, puffed in the massed ranks of the Hollerton Town Band, triple-tongueing his silver cornet with unrehearsed alacrity. Robert Snell sat, obsequiously efficient, at the gate attending to the ticket counting, while sequin-lidded Lynda, in the guise of Madame Za Za, lured unsuspecting victims to her tarot telling tent. Tony Archer, swilling beer, oversaw the wooden ball-throwing for hairy coconuts and pink pigs, while pinafored Phil and Brian manfully tended the hissing copper urn in the crowded tea tent.

PAT'S ALMOND LOAF

There are always eggs and yoghurt in abundance at Bridge Farm. This tea-time treat makes good use of these and is perfect for offering to visiting family and friends with an afternoon mug of tea.

½tsp bicarbonate of soda
5fl oz (¼pt/150ml) plain yoghurt
4oz (115g) butter or margarine
4oz (115g) caster sugar
2 large size eggs, separated
1tsp almond essence
6oz (170g) self-raising flour
2oz (55g) ground almonds

FOR THE TOPPING
3tbsp icing sugar
3–4tbsp hot water
1tsp flaked and toasted almonds

Add the bicarbonate of soda to the yoghurt, mix well and set to one side.

Grease and line a 2lb (900g) loaf tin.

Cream the butter and sugar until pale and fluffy. Add the beaten egg yolks and almond essence, then fold in the flour, ground almonds and yoghurt. Whisk the egg whites until stiff but not dry, then fold into the cake mixture. Put into the loaf tin. Bake in the centre of the oven at 350°F/180°C/Gas 4 for 50 minutes, then turn out on to a wire rack to cool.

To make the topping, mix the icing sugar with the water and spread over the top of the cake with a palette knife. Sprinkle with the almonds.

BAKER'S FLOOR CAKE

Rumour has it that this was the cake made from the sweepings at the end of the day in Doughy Hood's bake house. What would health and safety say about that now?

2oz (55g) chopped walnuts
2oz (55g) chopped dates
2oz (55g) halved cherries
1oz (25g) mixed peel
2 medium size eggs
4oz (115g) self-raising flour
5oz (140g) sugar
a pinch of cinnamon and mixed spice

Mix all the fruit together in a bowl with the beaten eggs. Add the sifted flour, sugar and spices and beat together thoroughly.

Spread the mixture into a greased, lined Swiss roll tin (approximately 7 x 11in (18 x 27cm)) and bake at 350°F/180°C/ Gas 4 for 40 minutes.

CLARRIE'S FAMOUS FRUIT CAKE

Everyone in Ambridge seems to know about Clarrie's fruit cake. Jethro used to take a good hefty slice of this for his 'elevenes' when he worked up at Brookfield.

4oz (115g) margarine or butter
5fl oz (¼pt/150ml) water
**1lb (450g) mixed fruit (currants,
    sultanas and peel)**
1tbsp chunky marmalade
2 medium size eggs
8oz (225g) plain flour
1tsp mixed spice
8oz (225g) soft brown sugar
½tsp bicarbonate of soda
1tsp vinegar

Melt the butter in a saucepan and add the water and mixed fruit. Bring to the boil and simmer for 5 minutes, then allow to cool.

Add the marmalade, beaten eggs, sifted flour and spice and sugar. Mix well and add the bicarbonate of soda dissolved in the vinegar.

Grease and line an 8in (20cm) cake tin and bake the mixture in this for approximately 1½hours at 350°F/180°C/Gas 4. Test with a skewer, which should come away clean when it's cooked.

Coffee Cake

rate — jrgs. 5 coffee cups of flour, 2 teasps. ~~teasps~~ *of cream of tartar, 2 teacups of sugar; Mix together thoroughly, then add 1egg, well beaten*

FREDA FRY'S VICTORIAN FAIRINGS

MAKES ABOUT 24

These are made as they were for fairs in Victorian times, according to Bert's wife...and who am I to argue?

4oz (115g) margarine or butter
1tbsp golden syrup
3oz (85g) brown sugar
6oz (170g) self-raising flour
½tsp bicarbonate of soda
1tsp ground ginger
½tsp ground mixed spice
pinch of salt

Melt the butter and syrup in a pan over a low heat and stir in the sugar. Remove from the heat and add the sieved flour, soda, spices and salt. Mix until a soft and smooth dough is formed.

Take rounded teaspoons of the mixture, roll into balls and place on greased baking trays, leaving room for the biscuits to spread.

Bake at 350°F/180°C/Gas 4 for 10–15 minutes before removing to a wire rack to cool.

COCONUT FLAPJACKS

MAKES 12–16 FINGERS

'A good standby to keep in the fridge or the larder', says Auntie Chris, 'just in case anyone bothers to call in for a cup of tea.'

4oz (115g) margarine
3oz (85g) golden syrup
4oz (115g) demerara sugar
6oz (170g) rolled oats
2oz (55g) desiccated coconut
1tsp almond essence

Melt the margarine, sugar and syrup together in a saucepan. Add the oats, coconut and almond essence and mix thoroughly.

Press the mixture into a shallow greased tin 9 x 6in (23 x 15cm) and bake in a preheated oven at 350°F/180°C/Gas 4 for about 30 minutes until golden.

Cool in the tin for 2–3 minutes before cutting into fingers. Allow to cool completely before removing.

MRS HORROBIN'S OAT CRUNCHIES

MAKES 12–16

Poor old Ivy's recipe. (I should think she's almost the only person in the village who still uses lard.)

3oz (85g) caster sugar
2oz (55g) lard
2oz (55g) margarine or butter
3tsp boiling water
1tsp golden syrup
a few drops of almond essence
2oz (55g) oats
4oz (115g) self-raising flour

Cream the sugar, lard and margarine together in a bowl. When pale and fluffy, beat in the hot water, syrup and almond essence. Then stir in the oats and flour and mix together thoroughly.

Take teaspoons of the mixture and roll into walnut-sized balls, and place on a greased baking tray. Leave space for the biscuits to spread.

Bake at 350°F/180°C/Gas 4 for 10–15 minutes. Allow to cool on a wire rack.

UNCLE WALTER'S WISDOM

'A swarm of bees in May
Is worth a load of hay.
A swarm of bees in July
Is not worth a butterfly.'

WATERCRESS SOUP

Elizabeth has found this recipe. Can't you just guess this was one of Julia's? For her the glass of gin was certainly not optional.

3 bunches watercress
2oz (55g) butter
2 medium onions, chopped
2 medium potatoes, chopped
20fl oz (1pt/600ml) chicken stock
  (or use a stock cube)
20fl oz (1pt/600ml) milk
salt and pepper
1 wine glass gin (optional)
4tbsp single cream

Wash the watercress well and discard any tough stalks.

Melt the butter in a large saucepan, add the roughly chopped onion and potato and cook gently for 5 minutes. Pour on the stock and add half the watercress and salt and pepper. Bring to the boil and simmer for 20 minutes.

Allow to cool and then purée in a food processor or blender until smooth. Add the remaining watercress and blend again to give a flecked appearance to the soup.

Return to the pan, add the milk and reheat gently. Adjust the seasoning.

To serve chilled, add a dash of gin and stir a swirl of cream into each portion.

SMOKED MACKEREL PÂTÉ

SERVES 6–8

A very special pâté when made with Auntie Pru's home-made horseradish cream recipe. Somewhat passé - but hey ho, it still tastes good.

3 large smoked mackerel
12oz (340g) curd cheese
1tbsp chopped parsley
finely grated zest and juice of 1 lemon
1oz (25g) softened butter
2tbsp horseradish cream
pepper and salt

Remove the skin and bones from the cooked mackerel. Add the cheese and mix thoroughly by hand, or in a blender or food processor.

Add all of the other ingredients to the mackerel and blend or stir the mixture thoroughly.

Pack into ramekin dishes or a large mould. Cover and refrigerate until required, but keep for two days at most.

Serve with hot toast and wedges of lemon.

HAM LOAF WITH GREEN PEPPERCORNS

SERVES 4–6

A fashionable picnic recipe in the nineteenth century, this conjures up wicker chairs and tables in the sun, and maids with wind-blown, beribboned caps. It must have come from Lower Loxley.

1lb (450g) cooked ham
4oz (115g) white breadcrumbs
1tsp (or more, according to taste) green peppercorns (the type in brine)
1tbsp finely chopped parsley
2 medium size eggs
5fl oz (¼pt/150ml) milk
mayonnaise for serving (optional)

Finely mince the ham (or chop in a processor) and mix with the breadcrumbs, parsley and peppercorns. Stir in the well beaten eggs and the milk.

Generously butter a 1½–2lb (675–900g) loaf tin. Press the mixture down into the tin and bake in a preheated oven at 300°F/150°C/Gas 2 for 50–60 minutes, or until set and lightly browned. Cool, then chill before slicing and serving.

It will keep for 3–4 days. If using as part of picnic fare, transport in the loaf tin.

SUNNY CARROT AND ORANGE SALAD

Brightly coloured and delicately flavoured, the mustard seeds make this salad special. Lynda says she enjoys this practically any time of the year.

1 tbsp olive oil
2 tsp black mustard seeds
4 oranges
2 lb (1 kg) young carrots
2 tsp chopped fresh parsley
2 oz (55 g) raisins

Heat the olive oil and fry the black mustard seeds until they pop, then allow to cool.

Squeeze the juice from one orange and add to the mustard seeds. Peel the other three oranges and segment them into pith-free pieces.

Scrub and coarsely grate the carrots. Combine all the ingredients and toss in the mustard seeds, olive oil and orange juice.

POTATO, WALNUT AND LOVAGE SALAD

SERVES 3

A mixed leaf salad of frisée, lamb's lettuce and rocket, washed and dried, is the ideal bed on which to serve this walnut-dressed potato salad. For the vegetarian add some macadamia nuts too.

1 lb (450 g) waxy new potatoes
  (Pink Fir Apple or Jersey Royals
  are ideal)
1 tbsp cider vinegar
salt, pepper and a pinch of sugar
1 tbsp walnut oil
1 tbsp light olive oil
1 tbsp lemon juice
1 tsp Dijon mustard
1 tbsp chopped walnuts
1 tbsp chopped lovage

Cook the cleaned, but not peeled, potatoes in boiling salted water, until just tender.

Mix the salt, pepper and sugar into the vinegar, then add all the other ingredients, except the walnuts and lovage. Mix thoroughly together.

Strain the potatoes and toss in the vinaigrette while still warm.

Add the walnuts and lovage to the salad when cool.

The vinaigrette may be stored in a screw-top jar in the refrigerator for 3–4 weeks. Shake well before use.

MEDITERRANEAN OLIVE PÂTÉ

A simple canapé and something a bit different from the rather tedious taramasalata. Spread on little salty biscuits.

7oz (200g) pitted black olives
2 anchovy fillets
2oz (55g) capers, rinsed
1 clove garlic
1tbsp lemon juice
pinch of chopped fresh
  (or dried) thyme
1tbsp brandy or rum
2tbsp olive oil
pinch of dry mustard
black pepper

Strain the black olives, if using tinned ones. Peel and chop the garlic, drain the anchovy fillets.

Put the olives, garlic, anchovies, capers, brandy, lemon juice and thyme into a liquidiser and blend to a rough paste. Stir in the olive oil and add the black pepper and mustard powder. Store in a screw-top jar for three days at the most.

Serve on strips of warm, crisp ciabatta if you can get it.

Make your own special Gentleman's Relish by combining a tin of anchovies with grated lemon zest. Pound in a mortar, adding a little vinegar and black pepper. Heat gently in a small pan. Pack in a small dish and refrigerate.

CREAMY RASPBERRY AND ALMOND TARTLETS

MAKES 6

Take the whipped cream and raspberries in separate containers and assemble at the picnic, serving the tartlets filled with the almond cream and topped with fresh raspberries. As part of a culinary feast, a cool-box is a must here! Make sure you're sitting comfortably before you start to eat these.

4oz (115g) butter
6oz (170g) plain flour
1½oz (40g) caster sugar
1½oz (40g) ground almonds
1 medium size egg yolk
water to mix
a few drops almond essence
10fl oz (½pt/300ml) double cream
1tbsp amaretto liqueur
1lb (450g) raspberries

Rub the butter into the flour, then add the sugar and ground almonds. Add the egg yolk and a little water with the almond essence to the dry ingredients, and mix until well amalgamated. Chill.

Roll out the pastry and line individual patty or bun tins, lining each one with foil and greasing well first. Bake blind at 375°F/190°C/Gas 5 for 10-15 minutes until they are pale biscuit colour. Cool a little before removing to a wire rack.

When cold, pack carefully into a tin or polythene container, ready for transportation.

Whip the cream, adding 1tbsp liqueur to give an almond flavour to the cream.

BAKED APRICOT CHEESECAKE

SERVES 6–8

This is a sumptuous cake to complement a mid-morning cup of coffee, especially when served with a dollop of cream whipped together with apricot brandy.

4oz (115g) dried apricots
  (ready soaked), chopped
3oz (85g) butter
4oz (115g) caster sugar
zest and juice of 1 lemon
10oz (280g) cream cheese
2 medium size eggs, separated
2oz (55g) ground almonds
1oz (25g) ground rice
a little icing sugar

Cream the butter, sugar and lemon zest together until pale and light. Add the sieved cream cheese and egg yolks, beating thoroughly. Stir in the ground almonds, ground rice, lemon juice and chopped apricots.

Whisk the egg whites until stiff and fold into the cheese mixture.

Turn into a greased and lined 8in (20cm) loose-bottomed cake tin and bake at 350°F/180°C/Gas 4 for 50–60 minutes.

Turn off the heat and leave the cheesecake to cool slowly in the oven.

WHOLEMEAL SCONES

These are delicious with Brookfield honey, or at breakfast with marmalade, but are at their very best eaten warm straight from the oven, and spread thickly with butter!

4oz (115g) plain flour
4oz (115g) wholemeal flour
1tsp bicarbonate of soda
pinch salt
2tsp cream of tartar
1½oz (40g) butter
2oz (55g) sultanas
¼tsp cinnamon
¼tsp powdered nutmeg
1 medium size egg
4tbsp milk, to mix

Sift the flours, bicarbonate of soda, salt and cream of tartar into a bowl, adding the bran left over in the sieve. Rub in the butter until the mixture resembles fine breadcrumbs. Stir in the sultanas, cinnamon and nutmeg.

Add the beaten egg to the milk and pour this into the centre of the flour mixture. Using the blade of a knife, mix into a rough dough. Knead lightly, then turn on to a floured surface and roll out until ½in thick. Using a 1½ in or 2in pastry cutter, stamp out the scones.

Put on greased baking trays and place in a hot oven at 425°/220°/Gas 7 for 10–15 minutes or until well risen.

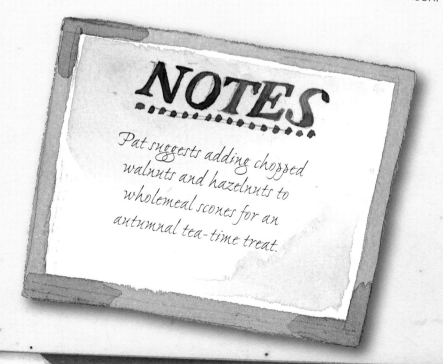

NOTES

Pat suggests adding chopped walnuts and hazelnuts to wholemeal scones for an autumnal tea-time treat.

CHEESE AND PRAWN MOUSSES

MAKES 6

These creamy little mousses can be eaten straight from the ramekins with a small spoon or fork. You can serve them with crudités too.

½oz (15g) gelatine
2tbsp water
1 clove garlic
1tbsp lemon juice
2fl oz (50ml) dry white wine
4oz (115g) Gruyère or cheddar cheese, grated
6oz (170g) shelled prawns (fresh or frozen)
8oz (225g) cream cheese
salt, pepper and pinch cayenne pepper
5fl oz (150ml/¼pt) double cream
basil leaves

Dissolve the gelatine in 2tbsp water. In a food processor or blender, blend the clove of garlic with the lemon juice and white wine. Add the grated cheese and prawns and blend until smooth. Add the cream cheese, gelatine and seasoning and blend again until well mixed.

Whip the cream until it stands in peaks, and fold into the cheese mixture.

Put into individual ramekin dishes, cover with cling film and chill. Decorate each mousse with a basil leaf. These can be made a day in advance and kept in the refrigerator.

TERRINE D'AVOCATS ET D'ASPERGES

This terrine of avocado and asparagus is a fresh, temptingly green starter. Sprinkle each slice liberally with freshly picked and chopped herbs, and serve a sharp mustardy vinaigrette with it.

12 plump asparagus spears
2 large avocados
juice of 1 lime
1oz (25g) gelatine
6fl oz (175ml) double cream
salt and freshly ground black pepper
Worcestershire or tabasco sauce,
  to taste (optional)

FOR THE VINAIGRETTE
4fl oz (125ml) olive oil
2tbsp white wine vinegar
½tsp caster sugar
2tsp Dijon mustard
salt and pepper

Trim the asparagus spears, discarding any tough, woody ends and knobbly lumps. Plunge into boiling salted water and cook gently until tender. Drain carefully.

Peel, stone and chop the avocados and put into a food processor or blender. Add the lime juice and purée until smooth, adding a little milk or cream if necessary.

In a basin, sprinkle the gelatine on to 3tbsp boiling water. Stir well and leave until dissolved.

In a saucepan, heat the cream until simmering – do not boil. Pour into the dissolved gelatine, stirring thoroughly, then sieve this creamy mixture into the avocado purée and season well, adding Worcestershire sauce or tabasco, if required.

Butter a 9in (23cm) terrine, or loaf tin, and line with cling film or baking parchment. Spread a shallow layer of avocado mixture on the bottom of the terrine and arrange the asparagus spears on this. Season with salt and freshly ground black pepper and cover with the remaining avocado mixture. Cover with cling film and refrigerate for 24 hours.

To serve, stand the terrine in a sink of hot water to loosen. Turn the avocado loaf out on to a serving plate and garnish with fresh herbs. Cut slices with a sharp-bladed knife which has been dipped in hot water.

To make the vinaigrette, place all the ingredients in a screw-top jar and shake well. More mustard can be added to make it thicker.

ANNABELLE'S TARTE À LA TOMATE

SERVES 4–6

'Just off for a little light lunch', Annabelle said as she nipped smartly past Brian and out of the office of Borchester Land.

9oz (250g) ready made puff pastry
5oz (140g) Boursin cheese
12oz (340g) cherry tomatoes
2tsp caster sugar
black pepper
a bunch of fresh basil

Roll out the pastry and line a 9in (23cm) loose-bottomed flan tin or oblong one of about 10 x 12in (25 x 30cm).

Fold the pastry edges in to make a border, prick the pastry with a fork and leave to chill.

Mash the Boursin cheese and spread over the pastry base.

Heat the olive oil in a pan and add the tomatoes, sprinkle on the sugar, and gently shake them around the pan to coat the skins. When the skins are beginning to split remove them from the heat and place them on the cheese. Grind some black pepper over them and bake the tart for 20 minutes at 180°C/(350°F/Gas 4), or until the pastry edges are puffy and golden. About halfway through the baking time add some torn basil leaves and return to the oven.

Serve warm with the remaining basil leaves to decorate.

PSYCHEDELIC SALAD

Using a colourful variety of edible flowers, as well as tender young leaves of dandelions, violets, sorrel and borage, Lynda creates a veritable kaleidoscope of a salad. On a large plate she arranges the fresh green leaves mingled with apple mint, fronds of fennel, mauve chive flowers, sprigs of curly parsley and marigold petals. A mild French dressing made from lemon juice, lime blossom honey and extra virgin olive oil is served separately.

QUICHE AUX FRUITS DE MER

Caroline also calls this a 'tarte' — well she would, wouldn't she? Serve hot or cold with a crispy green salad in a lemony dressing.

6oz (170g) shortcrust pastry
2tbsp chopped shallots
1½oz (40g) butter
4oz (115g) prawns,
　fresh or frozen
2oz (55g) tinned crabmeat
2tbsp white wine
salt and black pepper
3 medium size eggs
6fl oz (175ml) single cream
1tbsp tomato purée
1oz (25g) Gruyère cheese,
　grated

Roll out the pastry and line a 9in (23cm) fluted flan tin. Cook the shallots in the butter until soft and transparent. Add the prawns and crabmeat and stir gently for 2 minutes. Add the wine and seasoning and heat gently until bubbling.

Beat the eggs together with the cream and tomato purée and gradually blend into the shellfish mixture. Adjust the seasoning. Pour the mixture into the flan tin and sprinkle the Gruyère cheese over it.

Bake in a preheated oven at 375°F/190°C/ Gas 5 for 25–30 minutes until puffy and brown.

ALICE'S EASY PEASY PASTA

Away at university, she promises me she's eating sensibly. She even makes enough to share with a chum. Oh dear, could this be Christopher?

7oz (200g) Fiorelli pasta
1 large garlic clove, crushed
1 large lemon
4tbsp crème fraîche
4oz (115g) smoked salmon slivers
a few sprigs of fresh parsley,
   stalks removed
freshly grated parmesan cheese
salt and pepper

Cook the pasta in boiling salted water according to the instructions.

Heat the crème fraîche and lemon zest over a low heat. Add the crushed garlic and season with plenty of pepper, then continue heating until hot and bubbly.

Drain the pasta and toss immediately with the sauce, adding the chopped parsley and salmon slivers. Stir well to coat, and serve immediately in warm bowls.

Scatter with the parmesan cheese and a fresh grinding of black pepper.

LEMON GINGER CHICKEN

Much, much better than dull 'chicken in a basket', this also goes well with rice. I think Jolene still has this on the menu at The Bull.

8 chicken joints, skinned
2oz (55g) plain flour
2tbsp olive oil
a knob of butter
1 large onion, chopped
1 green pepper, deseeded
  and chopped
1 clove garlic, crushed
1in (5cm) piece of fresh root ginger,
  peeled and finely chopped
4oz (115g) mushrooms, sliced
grated zest of 1 lemon
10fl oz (½pt/300ml) dry white wine

Dust the chicken joints in flour. Heat the oil and butter in a large frying pan and fry the joints until browned. Transfer them to an ovenproof dish.

Put the onion and green pepper into the pan and sauté for a few minutes. Add the garlic, ginger, mushrooms and lemon zest and then gradually stir in the wine. Bring to the boil and pour the vegetable mixture over the chicken.

Place in a medium oven at 375°F/190°C/Gas 5 for 30–40 minutes.

Serve with a crisp green salad and French bread.

SPICY RICE

Nutty, glossy and golden, almost a meal in itself. With some prawns scattered over it, it could be just that. I almost prefer cashew nuts in place of almonds.

2tbsp cooking oil
1oz (25g) butter or margarine
2 medium onions, finely chopped
2 cloves garlic, crushed
1tsp ground cumin
1tsp ground coriander
1tsp ground cinnamon
1tsp turmeric
12oz (340g) long-grain, easy-cook rice
12fl oz (350ml) vegetable stock
salt and white pepper
6oz (170g) almond flakes, toasted

Melt the oil and butter in a large, heavy-bottomed pan and fry the onion until soft and golden. Add the garlic and all the spices and continue frying for another minute or two.

Stir in the rinsed rice and add the vegetable stock. Season with salt (not too much if the stock is already salty) and pepper, cover the pan with a well-fitting lid and simmer gently for 10-12 minutes, until all the liquid has been absorbed and the rice is cooked.

Stir in the freshly toasted almonds, transfer to a serving dish and serve hot or cold.

GOOSEBERRY FOOL

Gooseberries were a favourite fruit in the nineteenth century and even now prove to be a popular dessert for a warm July day. 'Top each with a sprig of mint', Mum says.

1lb (450g) ripe gooseberries,
  topped and tailed
6oz (170g) caster sugar
2 elderflower heads (optional)
8fl oz (225ml) double cream, whipped
grated zest of 1 small orange

Put the gooseberries and sugar in a pan, cover and simmer for 10–15 minutes until tender. (One or two heads of elderflower, tied in a muslin cloth, can be boiled with the gooseberries to counteract the acidity.) Allow to cool.

Put through a blender or rub through a sieve. Then fold in the cream and grated orange zest.

Spoon into individual dishes, chill and serve with wafer-thin biscuits.

Make elderflower vinegar by steeping rinsed and shaken elderflowers in white wine vinegar, then strain through a muslin cloth.

ELDERFLOW...

25 HEADS - ELDERFL...
20g (55G) TARTARI...
4 ORANGES SLICE...
1 LEMON SLIC...
3 lbs SUGAR
3 pints - BOIL BOIL...

Pick "Heads" when...

NANNY PARGETTER'S ORANGE SEED CAKE

*'Nanny always insisted we had this for nursery tea on Sundays',
confides Nigel, 'she never knew how much I hated those wretched
caraway seeds. And what's more Lily and Freddy do too!'*

6oz (170g) butter
12oz (340g) caster sugar
2tsp caraway seeds
4 medium size eggs
1lb (450g) self-raising flour
grated zest and juice of 1 orange

Cream the butter and sugar together until light and fluffy and add the caraway seeds. Beat in the eggs and gradually sift in the flour. Add the orange juice and grated zest and mix to a batter-like consistency.

Place the mixture in a greased and lined 8in (20cm) cake tin and bake in a preheated moderate oven at 350°F/180°C/Gas 4 for 1½–2 hours. Leave in the tin for a few minutes before turning out on to a wire rack to cool.

Store in an airtight container.

EARL GREY FRUIT CAKE

SERVES 2—3

Lady Goodman kindly gave this recipe to me one evening when she and Sir Sidney were having dinner with us. It's moist and delicately flavoured with oil of Bergamot, just the cake to impress a visiting great-aunt at tea on a summer's day.

2oz (55g) Earl Grey tea
10oz (280g) sultanas
10oz (280g) currants
4oz (115g) margarine
3oz (85g) butter
7oz (200g) soft dark brown sugar
3 medium size eggs
7oz (200g) self-raising flour
2oz (55g) ground almonds
4oz (115g) glace cherries, halved
4oz (115g) mixed peel
4oz (115g) walnuts, halved

Cream the margarine, butter and sugar. Add the eggs slowly and, with the last one, add a little flour. Fold in the rest of the flour, ground almonds, cherries, mixed peel, walnuts and the tea-soaked fruit.

Grease and line an 8in (20cm) cake tin and bake in a preheated oven at 300°F/150°C/Gas 2 for 3–3¼ hours. Test with a skewer, which should come away clean. Cool in the tin before turning out on to a wire rack.

Infuse tea in 10fl oz (½pt/300ml) boiling water for 1 hour, then drain. Soak the sultanas and currants in the tea mixture for at least 9 hours.

CHILLED STRAWBERRY PIMM'S

On a warm summer's evening what could be more perfect than a refreshing glass of chilled fruit Pimm's? Strawberries kindly donated by Adam, of course.

1 bottle Pimm's No 1
8oz (225g) strawberries,
   hulled and halved
Half a small cantaloupe melon,
   deseeded and chopped
1 orange, thinly sliced
a few fresh sprigs of mint
1 bottle lemonade
ice cubes

Pour the Pimm's into a jug. Add the strawberries, melon and orange slices. When ready to serve pour into tall glasses and add ice cubes, lemonade and top with a sprig of mint.

ELDERFLOWER PETILLANT

The Snells find this fun to make and even more fun to drink. It's so lively and potent it needs re-corking every day! To stop the constant popping, Robert expertly wires the corks in place.

12 large heads of elderflowers
   in full bloom
zest and juice of 2 lemons
1 gallon (4.5l) fresh spring water
1lb (450g) granulated sugar
3–4tbsp white wine vinegar

Shake and rinse the flower heads to remove any insects. Immerse the elderflowers in the cold spring water and add the sugar, vinegar and lemon zest and juice. Leave for 48 hours.
Strain the liquid carefully through a muslin cloth.
Bottle and cork, storing in a cool place for two weeks before using.

BRIE AND WALNUT TART

This is Elizabeth's favourite. I think she suggested it should be served in The Orangery at Lower Loxley.

FOR THE PASTRY
6oz (170g) plain white flour

pinch of salt

3oz (85g) butter or margarine

1 medium size egg yolk

water to mix

FOR THE FILLING
6oz (170g) Brie cheese

juice of half a lemon

2oz (55g) chopped walnuts

3 medium size eggs

10fl oz (½pt/300ml) single cream

salt and pepper

To prepare the shortcrust pastry, sieve the flour and salt into a mixing bowl. Cut the butter into cubes and rub lightly into the flour with the fingertips until it resembles fine breadcrumbs.

Beat the egg yolk with a little water and mix into the flour with a knife to make a soft dough. Turn on to a floured surface and roll out to the required thickness.

Line a 9in (23cm) flan tin with the pastry and bake blind in a moderately hot oven 375–400°F/190–200°C/Gas 5–6 for 15–20 minutes.

For the filling, soak the sliced Brie in lemon juice for half an hour. Place the cheese and the walnuts in the base of the flan case. Whisk the eggs and cream together and season well. Pour into the flan and bake in a preheated oven at 325°F/160°C/Gas 3 for 45 minutes, or until the filling is light and puffy and browned all over.

APPETIZERS

BAY LEAV

Tomato Juice
Aspic

SOUPS

Vegetable
Stock
Herb Bouquet
Fish Chowders

FISH

Pickled Fish
Crab
Shrimp

EGGS &
CHEESE

MEATS

Beef
Veal
Stews
Lamb
Pot Roast
Boiled Ham
Shish Kebab

POULTRY
& GAME

Boiled Chicken
Wild Game
Fricassee
Stews

VEGETABLES

Onions
Boiled Potatoes
Green Beans
Carrots
Eggplant
Stewed Tomatoes

SALADS

Fish
Aspic

SAUCES

All Marinades

DESSERTS
&
BEVERAGES

CREAMY PIQUANT CHICKEN

SERVES 4

Helen is delighted that this can be made with her tangy Borsetshire Blue. It's delicious served with a tossed salad.

4 chicken breasts, skinned and boned
1¼lb (500g) small waxy new potatoes
4oz (115g) butter
3 plump garlic cloves, crushed
4 fl oz (100ml) dry white wine
4 fl oz (100ml) vegetable stock or
  bouillon
4oz (115g) Blue Stilton or
  Roquefort cheese
4 fl oz (100ml) crème fraîche
salt and freshly ground black pepper

Cut each chicken fillet into large chunks. Scrub and rinse the new potatoes.

Melt the butter in a frying pan, add the chicken pieces and toss in the foaming butter until golden on all sides. Lift onto crumpled kitchen paper.

Toss the potatoes in the buttery juices in the pan until they take on a little colour.

Transfer potatoes and chicken into casserole dish.

Stir the garlic into the hot pan, then add the wine and the vegetable stock.

Pour the contents of the pan into the casserole dish and bake in the oven for 30–35 minutes at 350°F/180°C/Gas 4.

Remove from oven, stir in the crumbled cheese and crème fraîche and return to oven for another 10 minutes until the cheese has melted in a creamy sauce, and season to taste.

RED LEAF SALAD WITH BALSAMIC DRESSING SERVES 4

leaves of lollo rossa and red romaine
1 small shallot, finely chopped
1tbsp balsamic vinegar
3tbsp walnut oil
3tbsp walnut oil
pinch of salt and caster sugar

Combine shallot, vinegar, oils, salt and sugar then shake or whisk together. Taste and adjust oil to vinegar if needed.

Toss the salad leaves to lightly coat them with the dressing.

BRUSCHETTE WITH GOAT'S CHEESE AND BASIL

SERVES 4

Robert admitted this was a favourite light supper snack in front of the television. Lynda wouldn't allow it if B & B guests were staying.

1 flat rustic-style country loaf (or ciabatta)
1 plump garlic clove
4tbsp extra virgin olive oil
6oz (170g) fresh goat's-milk cheese
a bunch of fresh basil leaves

Split the loaf horizontally and cut into 2in strips. Arrange on a baking-sheet and grill the slices, inner surface uppermost, until they are just starting to brown.

Crush the garlic cloves into the olive oil and, while the bread is still warm, brush the top of the strips generously with oil and top with slices of goat's cheese.

Place under a hot grill briefly before serving. Decorate with basil leaves.

PRAWN DIP WITH CRUDITÉS

SERVES 6–8

So quick and easy to prepare, this dip is an old favourite with all at Home Farm. If you haven't time to make the mayonnaise, buy a good quality creamy one and add an extra squeeze of lemon juice.

6oz (170g) prawns, frozen or fresh
6tbsp mayonnaise
3tbsp milk
1½oz (40g) cheddar cheese,
  cut into cubes
1 small onion, chopped
1tsp Worcestershire sauce

Combine all the ingredients in a food processor or blender until smooth.

Serve with crudités – raw vegetables suitable for dipping into such sauces. Try carrot, celery, courgettes, celeriac and sweet peppers cut into little sticks, and cauliflower into small florets.

CRISP COURGETTE AND AUBERGINE MATCHSTICKS

SERVES 4

These are a wonderful accompaniment to crispy chicken or served as a starter dredged with grated parmesan cheese.

4oz (115g) plain flour
10fl oz (½ pint/300ml) sparkling water
1tbsp chopped fresh parsley or chervil
1 medium aubergine and 2 medium
  courgettes, cut into 1in (2cm) long
  matchsticks
oil, enough for deep frying
salt

Whisk the flour into the water to make a batter and let the mixture stand.

Heat the oil until it's just beginning to smoke, keeping a close eye on it all of the time.

Drop the 'chips' of aubergine and courgettes into the batter, and then fry until crisp and golden. Drain on absorbent kitchen paper and sprinkle with the parsley or chervil and salt.

COQUILLES ST JACQUES AUX POIREAUX

If you're invited to dinner at Caroline and Oliver's, I think this could well be on the menu. Delicately creamy and utterly delicious. For a fish course the scallops are served daintily in their shells.

12oz (340g) thin young leeks
2oz (55g) butter
8–12 scallops, shelled and cleaned
2 shallots, finely chopped
4fl oz (100ml) dry white wine
10fl oz (½pt/300ml) double cream
pinch of cayenne
freshly ground nutmeg (optional)
salt and freshly ground black pepper

Cut off the green parts of the leeks and discard. Split the white parts in half, lengthways. Trim and rinse thoroughly under the tap, then drain and cut into narrow strips 2in (5cm) long.

Melt 1oz (25g) butter with 2fl oz (60ml) water in a heavy-bottomed saucepan over a low heat. Add the leeks, cover and simmer for 15 minutes, stirring from time to time. When soft, remove from the heat and keep hot.

Rinse the scallops under cold, running water, removing any black threads. Cut the scallops in half horizontally.

Melt the remaining butter in a small pan, add the finely chopped shallots and cook until soft.

Add the scallops with their corals and the white wine. Bring to the boil and simmer gently for 2–4 minutes, depending on the size of the scallops. (Do not overcook as the corals will be damaged and the white flesh toughened.) Remove the scallops and keep warm with the leeks.

Increase the heat to reduce the cooking juices from the scallops and the leeks to half, then add the cream. Bring to the boil briefly and season to taste with salt and cayenne.

Serve the scallops on a bed of leeks. Pour over the cream sauce and sprinkle with nutmeg if required. Serve any extra sauce separately.

GOOSEBERRY SORBET

A sharp, refreshing sorbet to cleanse the palate. It is particularly attractive when made with pink gooseberries. 'The trouble with gooseberries is mould', Bert always mutters. But don't let him put you off!

12oz (340g) gooseberries
8oz (225g) caster sugar
grated zest and juice of 1 lemon
20fl oz (1pt/570ml) water
2 medium size egg whites

Rinse the gooseberries thoroughly but do not top and tail them. Place them in a pan with the sugar, lemon zest and juice and water. Bring this slowly to the boil and simmer for 10 minutes. Then pass the cooked fruit through a sieve and allow to cool.

Whisk the egg whites until stiff and beat them into the purée. Place in a freezer container and freeze for 2–3 hours, or until almost solid.

Remove from the freezer and beat thoroughly to break down the ice crystals. Return to the freezer for 1–2 hours until completely set.

A lump of sugar in the water will keep cut flowers fresh.

MIDSUMMER PUDDING

Having frozen a mélange of midsummer fruits, Lynda likes nothing better than to astonish her guests with this pudding in the depths of winter. 'It conjures up the magic of those warm evenings, Robert and I sitting on the terrace sipping chilled Chardonnay', she crows.

1½lb (675g) mixed red fruits, preferably strawberries, raspberries and redcurrants

4oz (115g) soft light brown sugar

8–10 thin slices of 2-day-old white bread, crusts removed (or to be extra special, bread made with egg, such as brioche or rich French bread)

Prepare the fruit, rinse and place in a heavy-bottomed saucepan. Add the sugar and heat gently for 5–8 minutes.

Line a 1½pt (850ml) pudding basin with the sliced bread, cutting a circle of bread to fit the base.

When the fruit is cooked, pour it carefully into the basin, reserving about 6tbsp of the syrup. When the basin is full, top with a layer of bread. Lay a plate or saucer that just fits inside the rim on top of the pudding, and place a weight on top of that. Leave overnight in the fridge.

To serve, run a knife around the edge to loosen and turn the pudding on to a serving dish.

Spoon over the remaining fruit juice and serve with dollops of crème fraîche or Greek yoghurt.

81
Summer

MISTY MEMORIES

AUGUST

Lower Loxley Hall

'Place the table over here, here in the deep green shade, where the cedar's shadows stretch dark and wide across the lawns. No, not by the house. The sun is so high and scorchingly hot – it's far too warm on the terrace too, it's toasting the stones and baking the terracotta pots. Oh the heat in this drought! The flowers are parched dry and drooping. They're just longing for a drop or two of rain or even a tiny taste of dew'.

Shallow china cups bedeck a pristine linen cloth. A stay-stiffened and superior lady perches on an upright bamboo chair. While at arm's length on a tartan rug sits a teddy bear and a floppy-bonneted, plump and propped-up baby Pargetter. Stamp-sized sandwiches are passed around. Fragrant tea is poured from a splendid silver pot. Just as the sharp, shiny blade cracks the crust on the Colonial cake, a jagged flash of lightning splits the darkened sky. A giant boom of thunder shakes the ground and big fat drops of rain begin to fall.

A brisk tap on the door disturbs my reverie. 'Jennifer, where on earth have you got to? There's a mug of tea for you on the kitchen table.' And then ... and then, I turn away, leaving my story's scene trapped, sepia-tinted, in its dusty ebony frame.

FRUIT BRULÉE

SERVES 3–4

A delicious and simple choice for entertaining in the summer when soft fruits are plentiful. Obviously we use strawberries.

1lb (450g) soft fruits (such as raspberries, mulberries, strawberries, blackcurrants)
3oz (85g) caster sugar
6fl oz (170ml) double cream
6fl oz (170ml) whole milk yoghurt
6oz (170g) demerara or soft brown sugar

Place the fruit in a saucepan over a moderate heat. Add the caster sugar and heat until the sugar has dissolved. Place in a shallow ovenproof dish and allow to cool.

Whip the cream until thick and then fold in the yoghurt. Spread this mixture carefully over the fruit right up to the edges of the dish. Thickly sprinkle the demerara sugar on top.

Preheat the grill to its highest setting and place the dish under for about three minutes, until the sugar is bubbling and caramelised.

Chill before serving.

NOTES

To crystallise grapes or edible flowers, such as violets and rose petals, paint with frothy beaten egg white and dust with caster sugar. Leave to dry and harden at room temperature.

ROSY RASPBERRY AND HAZELNUT ROULADE

SERVES 6–8

Serve with a glossy chocolate sauce (see opposite). Too rich and fattening for me, though — I'd rather make a sharp raspberry coulis to go with it.

4 medium size eggs
4oz (115g) caster sugar
3oz (85g) ground toasted hazelnuts
1tsp baking powder
a little icing sugar
6fl oz (175ml) double cream
2tbsp framboise liqueur (optional)
8oz (225g) fresh raspberries, and a few for decoration

Grease a 12 x 8in Swiss roll tin and line with baking parchment.

Whisk the eggs and sugar in a bowl placed over a pan of hot water, until pale and thick.

Gently fold in the ground toasted hazelnuts and sifted baking powder. Spread the mixture in the prepared tin and bake for 15 minutes at 400°F/200°C/Gas 6. Allow the cake to cool in its tin.

Place a piece of greaseproof paper dredged with icing sugar on the work surface. Turn out the cake, having first loosened the edges with a palette knife, and trim off the crisp edges.

Whip the cream until stiff, gradually adding the liqueur, and then spread it over the cake with a palette knife. Scatter some of the raspberries over and then, using the greaseproof paper to help, roll up the cake like a Swiss roll. Don't worry if the surface of the roulade cracks — it actually adds to the delicious homemade appearance.

Transfer to a serving dish. Decorate with the remaining raspberries and liberally sprinkle with icing sugar. Chill in the fridge for at least 2 hours before serving.

CHOCOLATE SAUCE

4oz (115g) good quality plain chocolate
3tbsp golden syrup
3fl oz (90ml) single cream

Break the chocolate into pieces and melt
over a bowl of hot water. Stir in the syrup.
   Heat the cream without boiling and
gradually stir into the chocolate mixture.
Flood plate with sauce and place the
roulade on top, if making a big impression.

RASPBERRY COULIS

12oz (340g) fresh raspberries (or frozen)
5oz (140g) caster sugar
juice of half a small lemon
1tbsp brandy

Put all the ingredients into a blender or
food processor. Blend together, then rub
through a fine sieve. Chill before serving.

Autumn

A hazy veil blots away the view of the meandering Am early this dew-logged morning. Old Bert Fry, wearing his woollen socks for the very first time since last winter, pushes his wheel-squeaking barrow to his precious vegetable patch. 'A hill full, a hole full. Bet yer cannot catch a bowl full' he muses, mournfully prodding the glowing, smouldering haulms of last season's long green runners. A spicy, nose-tickling plume twists and spirals high, to just a whisp of mist through the towering beech. Tall bamboo canes, raffia tied and neatly stacked, stand ready for next year's rampant climbing feast. Proudly ranged on his old shed roof are robust rows of gleaming gold, plump matt pumpkins. Compost-nourished, keenly nurtured and ripening now in autumn's ochre sunshine, they patiently await their proud presentation at St Stephen's Harvest Home.

Down the narrow grey thread of a lane towards Traitor's Ford old Gran Archer, fruited loaf in a linen-covered willow woven basket beside her, would trot along in her pony- trap to visit old friends. Here now are the same wild hedgerows, speckled with blood-bright berries. Tawny hawthorns and orange-pink spindle are tangled and entwined with

old man's beard – wild birds'
winter feast. At tempting
tiptoe height, where
tortoiseshells hover
and flutter, are the
biggest, juiciest, lip-
staining, just-right-
for-picking blackberries
– beggars' harvest.

Fields have turned from gold to
stubble-stippled brown. In the misty
distance, over towards Heydon Berrow,
a tractor moans; no longer Blossom and Boxer, with their
huge and frilly feet, plodding heavily along the Brookfield furrows.
The tractor comes in sight, bright toy-town blue, glinting and gleaming
in the shafts of sunlight. Wheeling clouds of rooks and gulls whirl and
swirl and follow the shining silver discs. No time to wait, no time to waste;
fields no longer left fallow for a fresh season and the crop's rotation.
No faith in nature now. The sun is sinking low with a rosy golden glow,
flooding the western skies. As the shimmering twilight creeps from the
east, a chattering, noisily squabbling, gathering of swallows collects in
agitated rows along the humming telegraph wire, wisely debating which
day to depart to warmer, kinder climes.

Deep in the ditch someone else has smelled the smouldering of wood
smoke, the nuttiness of the woodland's decaying leaves, the musky
mellowness of autumn. This bright-eyed hedgehog has curled himself
up into a spiny, spiky ball, rolled himself in a blanket of beech leaves and
now just dreams of worms and snails and a slug-rich spring.

MISTY MEMORIES

SEPTEMBER

Ambridge Flower & Produce Show

Inside the hall there was an air of teasing smells and tempting success, and Ambridge's cottagers were milling and babbling with excitement. Standing neatly on trestle tables, pinned with paper cloths, were bottles and jars in rank and file, obeying judges' orders. All were clearly labelled: sherbert-bright lemon curd, tawny, chunky marmalade, rose-red jam. Golden Madeira cakes sat trapped under clingy-clear food-wrap awaiting the judges' knife-sharp incision, their crumby-lipped decision. Vivid spears of gladioli towered above vulgar pompom dahlias and jars of unassuming Michaelmas daisies. In dumpy pottery pots and earthenware mugs were the children's treasures – unpretentious posies, wind-blown flowers from wood and hedgerow, all instantly appealing in their innocent simplicity.

FIRST PRIZE
Awarded to:
....
For: WILD FLOWER POSY

MADEIRA CAKE

All candidates entering the Madeira cake class in the Fruit, Flower & Produce Show should follow this recipe.

6oz (175g) butter, softened
6oz (175g) caster sugar
3 medium size eggs, beaten
grated zest of 1 lemon
8oz (225g) plain flour
2tsp (level) baking powder
milk and water to mix
2 strips lemon peel

Cream the butter and sugar together until pale and fluffy. Add the eggs and lemon zest and beat again. Stir in the sifted flour and baking powder alternately with the milk and water. Mix thoroughly.

Put into a greased and lined 7in (18cm) round cake tin and bake in the oven at 350°F/180°C/Gas 4. After 30 minutes place the citron peel on the mixture and continue to bake for a further 1– 1½ hours until cooked. (Test with a skewer, which should come away clean.)

Turn the cake out and allow to cool on a wire rack.

MARROW, LEMON AND GINGER JAM

This syrupy, lumpy jam can be used in tarts and pastry dumplings. It was one of Martha Woodford's recipes. 'My Joby loves my dumplings', she'd always say.

3lb (1.5kg) marrow
3lb (1.5kg) granulated or
  preserving sugar
juice and grated zest of 3 lemons
1tsp ground ginger
4oz (115g) crystallised ginger, chopped

Peel, seed and chop the marrow into 1in (2cm) dice. Weigh, and place in a bowl. Measure the same weight of sugar, and add two-thirds to the marrow. Leave overnight.

Transfer to a preserving pan, add the lemon zest and juice, bring to the boil and cook for 30 minutes.

Add the remaining sugar and ginger and boil gently until setting point is reached and the marrow is transparent. Pot, seal and label.

To remove the scum from the surface of freshly boiled jam or marmalade either drop in a knob of butter or blot with sheets of kitchen roll.

CLARRIE'S CRUNCHY CHUTNEY

In the warmth of Clarrie's kitchen, with a jug of cider at his elbow, Joe revels in a hunk of Lizzie Larkin's Loaf, (see page 160) a chunk of strong cheddar and a spoonful of his favourite chutney. The delight of this is that it needs no cooking.

1lb (450g) dates
1lb (450g) sultanas
1lb (450g) apples, unpeeled,
  cored and chopped
1lb (450g) onions
1lb (450g) dark brown moist sugar
20fl oz (1pt/600ml) malt vinegar
1tsp salt
½tsp ginger
1tsp dry mustard

Mince the dates and sultanas, cored apples and peeled onions. Put in a large bowl with the sugar, vinegar and spices and stir thoroughly. Leave for 24 hours stirring occasionally.

Pot in clean jars, label and seal.

CAROL TREGORRAN'S BRANDIED APRICOT AND ALMOND CONSERVE

Dear John. Oh how I miss the Tregorrans! This can be used as an instant dessert with fromage frais and a finger of shortbread. Conserves have a 'softer' set than jams.

2lb (1kg) dried apricots
80fl oz (2.3litres/4pt) water
4 lemons
4lb (2kg) preserving sugar
3½oz (100g) flaked almonds
5fl oz (¼pt/140ml) brandy

Soak the dried apricots in water overnight. Strain the fruit and reserve the liquid. Roughly chop the fruit. Pour this liquid into a preserving pan with the grated zest of the four lemons and the sugar. Simmer gently until the sugar has dissolved, then boil until the syrup has thickened and reduced by about one-third.

Cut away all the pith from the lemons with a sharp knife, slice them thinly and put into the syrup with the apricots. Return to the boil, and simmer until the apricots are tender. Stir in the flaked almonds and brandy.

Stand for 1 hour, then pour into warm clean jars. Seal and label.

As conserves do not keep as well as jams, it is wise to check them from time to time. Once opened, keep in a refrigerator.

Auntie Pru said that cane sugar is better than beet sugar when jam-making, and always to use a wooden spoon.

SPICED HEDGEROW JELLY

On a mellow September afternoon, the bees humming dozily and drunkenly on the ripe fruit, Clarrie says she finds it peaceful and relaxing to pick berries for her jam-making. I don't know how she finds the time. This jelly is good in puddings or with cold meat.

3lb (1.4kg) blackberries
3lb (1.4kg) elderberries
1tsp cloves, tied in muslin
2 lemons
20fl oz (1pt/600ml) water
sugar (see below for quantity)

Pick over and clean up the blackberries. Strip the elderberries from their stalks and wash them. Put the fruit in the preserving pan with the cloves. Add the juice of the lemons and water. Bring slowly to the boil and simmer for 45 minutes, bruising the fruit with a wooden spoon until all the juice has run out. Remove the bag of cloves and strain the fruit through a muslin cloth or jelly bag.

Measure the juice and weigh out the sugar, allowing 12oz (340g) for each pint of juice.

Return the juice to the clean pan and boil for 15 minutes.

Add the warmed sugar, stir until it dissolves and then bring to the boil. Boil fast for about 10 minutes or until the jelly sets.

NOTES

To add a delicate flavour to apple purée or jelly, add a scented pelargonium leaf when boiling the apples.

Bottling Fresh Fruits

Choice

Use chutneys to make a quick spicy sauce by he with a little stock, to se with chops, or add to meat dishes and curry

TIPS FOR CHU

The fruit and vegetab chutney may be bruised a ever mouldy or rotten, as flavour and keeping quali Always cut away nasty pa

2. The vinegar and su chutney so always use th mended in the recipe. brown sugar produce chutney whereas granula distilled vinegar give a li The flavour of the ch slightly different depen sugar and vinegar used.

3. With vinegar mixtu aluminium or stainless copper or brass one.

4. Most chutneys are ce

Ripe Red Toma

SPICY SEPTEMBER CHUTNEY

A perennial favourite which Gran Archer used to make years ago — and so did Auntie Pru. 'Always use sound, ripe fruit gathered on a dry day' the recipe says, written in a faint sloping hand.

3lb (1.4kg) cooking apples
1lb (450g) pears
2lb (1kg) tomatoes
1lb (500g) chopped dates
2lb (1kg) granulated or
 brown sugar
1tsp cayenne pepper
2tsp mixed spice
1tsp cinnamon
1tsp ginger
1tsp salt
20fl oz (1pt/600ml)
 malt vinegar

Peel, core and chop the apples and pears.

Skin, deseed and chop the tomatoes.

Put the apples, pears, tomatoes and remaining ingredients into a large pan and bring to the boil. Simmer gently until the fruit and vegetables are tender and the chutney is thick, with no liquid lying on the top.

Pour into clean, warm jars, filling right to the top. When cold, cover and label.

OCTOBER

Harvest Supper

'Come, ye thankful people come' – to the annual harvest supper in the village hall, the third week of pheasant-shooting, nut-picking, leaf-dropping October. On the window ledge the russet Ribston pippins, mottled and plump, were spaced, along with other fruits picked specially from Ambridge orchards. Bronze chrysanthemums, eternally autumnal, were interspersed with crusty, corn-shaped cottage loaves along the laden linen-covered tables. The fresh-faced Ambridge farming folk sat amicably together, and fraternally side-by-side. They raised their effervescent glasses to thirsty lips, cleared their dusty throats and praised the Lord (and the PCC) for 'harvest-home'.

KEEPER'S COTTAGE CASSEROLE

SERVES 4–5

One day Clarrie carried to Keeper's Cottage a basket full of Tony's organic vegetables. 'I'm lucky; they were a bit damaged and couldn't be sold. Pat gave me the recipe too.'

4oz (115g) lentils
2tbsp vegetable oil
2 onions, peeled and finely chopped
2 cloves garlic, peeled and chopped
2 sticks celery, finely chopped
3 small turnips, chopped into small cubes
4 carrots, diced
4 leeks, cleaned and sliced
2 parsnips, diced
20fl oz (1pt/600ml) vegetable or chicken stock
1tbsp parsley
1tbsp dried mixed herbs
salt and pepper

Soak the lentils in cold water overnight, then drain.

Heat the oil in a frying pan and sauté the onion, garlic and celery until slightly browned.

Add the root vegetables and cook for 5 minutes, turning them in the oil. Add the lentils to the frying pan with the stock and stir over a low heat until simmering. Add the herbs and salt, pour into a casserole, cover and cook for 1–1½ hours in a low oven at 300°F/150°C/Gas 2.

Remove the lid for the last 15 minutes of cooking and scatter a mixture of wholemeal breadcrumbs, grated cheese and herbs on the top. This forms a delicious crumbly crust.

Serve with hot baked potatoes and a green vegetable.

INDIAN SPICED LAMB WITH RAITA

SERVES 2–3

Kenton has become a dab hand at making a meal for Kathy. He keeps the curry slowly cooking in the oven while he nips out for a game of poker.

3tbsp cooking oil
2 medium onions, finely chopped
1lb (450g) fillet of lamb, trimmed and
   cut into bite-size pieces
1tsp chilli powder
½ inch (1cm) piece fresh root ginger,
   peeled and chopped
3 cloves garlic, peeled and chopped
1½tsp turmeric
1½tsp ground coriander
½tsp cumin seeds
½tsp garam masala
4fl oz (110ml) yoghurt
4fl oz (110ml) water
salt

FOR THE RAITA
8fl oz (½pt/225ml) plain yoghurt
6oz (175g) cucumber, chopped, or
   coarsely grated and squeezed dry
1tbsp freshly chopped mint
salt and pepper

Heat the oil in a heavy-based saucepan and fry the onions until soft but not brown. Remove to a plate.

Fry the lamb, stirring and turning until browned. Remove to the plate.

Put the chilli powder, ginger, garlic and all the other spices into the pan. Stir in the yoghurt and water and bring to simmering point.

Return the lamb and onions to the pan, add salt and simmer the curry slowly for 40–50 minutes.

To make the raita, mix all the ingredients together and serve in a separate bowl. A pinch of crushed coriander can be added for a spicier taste.

Serve with raita and rice, with naan bread to soak up the sauce.

UNCLE WALTER'S WISDOM
'No matter how humble, how rough or how rude, A man should be willing to show gratitude.'

HARVESTER'S RABBIT WITH SAGE DUMPLINGS

SERVES 4–6

A different recipe from an ordinary rabbit casserole, but Joe isn't keen on the 'fancy' orange slices. So Clarrie promises next time she'll put in some chopped streaky bacon instead. 'Oh Joe, stop moanin!'

1 skinned rabbit, cut into 6 portions
a little flour
oil or butter for frying
2 onions, sliced
10fl oz (½pt/300ml) brown ale
1 orange, scrubbed and thinly sliced
1tsp mixed herbs
salt and black pepper

FOR THE DUMPLINGS

4oz (115g) self-raising flour
2oz (55g) shredded suet
1tbsp freshly snipped sage
1tbsp freshly snipped chives
salt and pepper
water to mix

Wash the rabbit portions, dry and toss in seasoned flour.

Heat the oil in a pan and fry the rabbit for a few minutes until brown, then transfer to a casserole.

Fry the sliced onions until transparent, then put with the rabbit.

Stir the ale into the residue in the pan and add the orange, herbs and seasoning. Reduce the liquid a little by boiling, then pour into the casserole. Cover the casserole and cook in a moderate oven at 350 °F/180°C/Gas 4 for 1½ hours.

Meanwhile, prepare the dumplings by mixing the flour, suet, herbs and seasoning thoroughly. Then add just enough water to make a firm dough. Turn on to a floured board, cut into pieces and roll into balls.

Drop these into the casserole 15 minutes before the end, replacing the lid.

TONY'S RICH RAGOÛT

*As soon as Tony realises the rich sauce is alcohol-based he's happy.
'Don't mention rich to me', he sighs. He enjoys a baked potato topped
with horseradish cream to accompany this dish.*

2lb (1kg) chuck or braising steak
2tbsp vegetable oil
large chopped onion
2tbsp plain flour
zest and juice of 1 orange
10fl oz (275ml/ ½pt) pale ale
1tbsp redcurrant jelly
1tbsp tomato purée
salt and pepper
bay leaf

Cut the meat into bite-size pieces and
fry in the oil, a few pieces at a time,
browning on all sides. Remove from
the pan and place in a casserole.

Fry the onion until soft and
transparent. Stir in the flour and cook
for 1 minute. Add the zest and juice of
the orange and the ale, stirring until it
comes to the boil. Stir in the redcurrant
jelly, tomato purée and seasoning.

Pour over the meat, add the bay leaf
and cook at 300°F/150°C/Gas 2 for
2– 2½ hours.

TOM ARCHER'S MUSTARD CRUSTED HAM

SERVES 8–10

This is perfect for a party if you're feeding a lot of people.

**2½–3lb (1.1–1.4kg)
 gammon or collar
2tbsp clear honey
2tbsp wine vinegar
2tbsp demerara sugar
2tbsp coarse-grain mustard**

Soak the bacon in a saucepan of cold water overnight to remove salt, changing the water to cook.

Weigh the joint to calculate the cooking time, allowing 25 minutes per lb (450g), plus 25 minutes. Cover and simmer for half the required cooking time.

Remove the bacon from the liquid. Wrap in foil and place in a roasting tin. Bake in the oven at 350°F/180 °C/Gas 4 until 30 minutes before the cooking time is complete.

Remove the foil, cut off the rind and score the fatty surface of the joint. Heat the honey and vinegar together and pour over the joint. Mix the sugar and mustard together and press into the surface of the ham where the rind has been removed.

Return to the oven at an increased temperature of 400°F/200°C/Gas 6 to finish cooking.

When cold, slice as thinly as possible.

UNCLE WALTER'S WISDOM
'Now wine, rum and whisky
are good if they're free
But there's value for money
in beer and in tea.'

TARTE AUX POMMES

I think everyone was bursting with enthusiasm after their visit to France many years ago. They were encouraged by Jean-Paul to try some simple French recipes. Here's one that they favoured for high days and holidays.

FOR THE PÂTÉ SUCREE
8oz (225g) plain flour
salt
6oz (175g) butter or margarine
1oz (25g) icing sugar
1 medium size egg yolk
1tbsp cold water

FOR THE FILLING
2lb (1kg) cooking apples
a little butter
4oz (115g) caster sugar
grated zest of 1 orange
grated zest of half a lemon

To make the pâté sucrée, sift the flour and salt together and mix in the butter, icing sugar and egg yolk with your fingertips, adding water if necessary. Knead the pastry until smooth, then wrap in polythene and chill for half an hour.

To make the filling, core the apples and slice, unpeeled, into a buttered pan. Cover and cook over a gentle heat until soft. Pass the apples through a sieve, adding the sugar and orange and lemon zest to the purée. Cook again until the purée thickens, then allow to cool.

Roll the pastry out thinly to line a 9in (23cm) flan tin, then bake blind at 400°F/200°C/Gas 6 for about 15 minutes, or until the pastry is set.

When cool, pile the cold apple mixture into the flan case and serve with whipped cream or yoghurt.

STRAWBERRY AND APPLE CRUMBLE WITH NUTTY TOPPING

An all-time favourite at Home Farm, this can be made with frozen fruit just as successfully as fresh. And it takes hardly any time to make the crumble in a food processor. Strawberries again!

4oz (115g) butter
6oz (175g) plain flour
2oz (55g) ground almonds
1oz (25g) chopped hazelnuts
1oz (25g) medium oatmeal
6oz (175g) demerara sugar
2lb (1kg) Bramley apples,
  peeled and cored
a little water
8oz (225g) late strawberries, with 2–3oz
  (55–85g) sugar or to taste

To make the crumble, rub the butter into the flour until it resembles fine breadcrumbs. Add the ground almonds, chopped hazelnuts, oatmeal and sugar and mix together well.

Thickly slice the apples into chunks and put into a large saucepan with a scant half cupful of water. Heat gently until the apples have begun to soften, then stir in the sugar and strawberries and remove from the heat.

Spoon the fruit into a large ovenproof dish. When cool, sprinkle the crumble mixture on to the fruit and lightly press it down. Place in a preheated oven at 350°F/180°C/Gas 4 and bake until golden-brown, about 40 minutes. Serve with dollops of Pat's creamy yoghurt.

Pat makes a special pastry for fruit pies using half margarine and half cream cheese. Mix with lemon juice and add a little water to make a soft dough with plain flour.

MISTY MEMORIES

November

Bonfire Party

The fields had turned from gold to brown; the fretwork of trees was silhouetted against the grey skies, and the sun hung like a feeble lantern trying in vain to prolong the short afternoon. For some weeks twigs, branches, sticks and boxes had been piling up Grundy-fashion in a growing stack on the village green. A breeze blew up – the bonfire hissed and crackled as flames leapt against the black velvet night. The spicy smell of wood smoke wafted towards us on the cold air. Eyes shone brightly in rosy faces glowing in the firelight. There were 'oohs' and 'aahs' as Catherine-wheels whirled and sparklers sparkled, whoops and squeaks as rockets exploded in myriad shimmering coloured stars. Sticky lips were licked, gooey toffee was sucked and chewed and steaming hot potatoes huffed and puffed on. The plump, misshapen figure of the guy was propped aloft, his sad, dejected form unnervingly familiar. Flames leapt around his straw-stuffed jeans, his jacket smouldered slowly. The freakish features on his stuffed-stocking face melted and twisted to a ghoulish grin. Then, as the fire engulfed him in a flaming orange furnace, he slumped forward in submission and showers of yellow sparks shot up into the sky.

GINGER PARKIN

This is Ruth's recipe, gleaned from her relations in the north. As she has more time than busy Ruth, Jill bakes it for bonfire night. For those with a sweet tooth it can be glazed with a layer of ginger icing.

10oz (275g) wholewheat or
  white self-raising flour
5oz (140g) coarse oatmeal
4oz (115g) demerara sugar
1tsp bicarbonate of soda
1tsp (heaped) ground ginger
1tsp allspice
4oz (115g) golden syrup or treacle
3oz (85g) lard
3oz (85g) margarine
a little milk

Mix the dry ingredients together in a bowl. In a saucepan melt the lard, margarine and syrup and stir into the dry ingredients. Stir until well mixed, adding enough milk to make a soft consistency.

Grease and line a 9in (23cm) square baking tin. Put the mixture in and bake in a moderate oven at 350°F/180°C/Gas 4 for about 1 hour, or until firm. Allow to cool before turning out.

This can be stored for up to a week in an airtight container before eating.

BONFIRE TOFFEE

MAKES ABOUT 1½LB

I remember Debbie made this sweet, bubbling recipe on the Aga at Home Farm years ago. It played havoc with Freda Fry's dentures!

12oz (340g) soft brown sugar
5oz (140g) butter
2tbsp golden syrup
2½ fl oz (⅛pt/75ml) water

Put all the ingredients in a heavy-bottomed saucepan and bring slowly to the boil, stirring constantly. After the sugar has dissolved, simmer steadily until a temperature of 290°F/140°C is reached on a sugar thermometer, or until a drop of toffee forms brittle threads when placed into a cup of cold water.

Pour into a greased tin, and mark into squares with a knife before completely set. When cold, pack in an airtight container.

BAKED POTATOES WITH SAVOURY BUTTERS

*Fireworks are finished but we're still gathering round the glowing fire.
The children think it's great fun to bake potatoes in the embers.*

Scrub baking-sized potatoes and cut a cross or slit on each one. Prick the skins, rub with coarse sea salt and olive oil and wrap each potato in kitchen foil. Cook in a preheated oven at 425°F/220°C/Gas 7 for 1½ hours.

When completely cooked, open up the foil and serve with a choice of savoury butters.

The following butters can be made a few hours beforehand and stored in the refrigerator. Allow 1oz (25g) of butter per person.

HERBED BUTTER

4oz (115g) softened butter
2tsp finely chopped fresh parsley
1tsp chopped fresh coriander
salt and pepper
a pinch of cayenne pepper

Pound the butter together with the herbs and seasoning until thoroughly mixed. Chill in a covered container until needed.

BLUE CHEESE BUTTER

4oz (115g) butter
2oz (55g) Roquefort or Danish
  blue cheese
1 clove garlic

Pound the butter together with the cheese and garlic until thoroughly mixed. Chill in a covered container until needed.

MUSTARD AND HORSERADISH BUTTER

4oz (115g) butter
2tsp coarse grain mustard
2tsp horseradish sauce

Pound the butter together with the mustard and horseradish sauce until thoroughly mixed. Chill in a covered container until needed.

LEEK AND POTATO SOUP

SERVES 6

This is great to serve either hot or chilled. It's one of Alan's favourite supper-time treats for Usha after a busy day with her clients.

2oz (55g) butter
2 onions, chopped
1lb (450g) leeks
1lb (450g) potatoes, diced
1tsp Dijon mustard
30fl oz (1½pt/900ml) chicken stock (or use a stock cube)
salt and pepper
5fl oz (¼pt/140ml) natural yoghurt or single cream
chopped fresh chives

Melt the butter in a large saucepan. Add the onions, roughly chopped leeks and potatoes. Toss in the butter and stir, cooking for 5 minutes. Add the mustard, stock and seasoning. Bring to the boil, then cover and simmer for 30 minutes.

Allow to cool slightly, strain off the liquid and either sieve the vegetables or put through a blender. Gradually mix the liquid into the purée.

When ready to serve add the cream or yoghurt and garnish with chopped chives.

PARSNIP, POTATO AND NUTMEG SOUP

SERVES 6—8

This is a heart-warming soup that Brian likes me to take out to the shoot in vacuum flasks on chilly days. He says it's improved enormously by the addition of a glass or two of good Amontillado!

2lb (1kg) parsnips, diced
2 large potatoes, chopped
3 large onions, chopped
40fl oz (2pt/1.2l) vegetable stock
salt and pepper
freshly grated nutmeg

Simmer the vegetables in 30fl oz (1½ pt/900ml) of the stock for about 35 minutes or until tender. Purée in a blender or food processor. Add the remaining stock, seasoning and a generous sprinkling of nutmeg.

Serve with hot garlic bread or granary rolls.

COURGETTE AND CELERY SOUP

SERVES 6

A late summer soup; I think all of Ambridge made this last year as Bert's vegetable plot was covered in courgettes.

8oz (225g) courgettes
1oz (25g) butter
3 celery sticks, trimmed and chopped
2 leeks, cleaned, trimmed and cut into
 ¼in (1cm) slices
1 large onion, chopped
1oz (25g) plain flour
40fl oz (2pt/1.2l) chicken stock
 (or use a stock cube)
2tbsp dry sherry
4fl oz (110ml) double cream
salt and pepper

Dice the topped and tailed courgettes.
 Melt the butter in a large saucepan over a moderate heat and fry the celery, leeks and onion until they have softened. When the onion becomes transparent, stir in the flour to make a paste. Gradually add the stock and sherry, stirring all the time. Add the diced courgettes, bring to the boil and simmer for 20 minutes.
 Purée in a blender or food processor and then stir in the double cream. Add salt and pepper to taste.

AUNT LAURA'S CURE FOR CREAKING JOINTS:

Boil 2lb (1kg) chopped celery in 80fl oz (2.3L/4pt) water until tender. Add 1l/2lb (675g) brown sugar and 1/4oz (5g) yeast, and then bottle.

PAT'S WALNUT BREAD

There's nothing to compare with Pat's Walnut Bread served warm, with a chunk of Helen's crumbly Borsetshire Blue.

(This recipe could also be used to make three round loaves. Place them on baking sheets and cook for 30–35 minutes)

1oz (25g) fresh yeast or 1tbsp easy-blend dried yeast
½tsp honey
20fl oz (1pt/600ml) approx warm water
2½lb (1.125kg) strong wholemeal flour
2tsp salt
8fl oz (225ml) plain yoghurt
4oz (115g) chopped walnuts

In a small bowl mix the yeast, honey and a little tepid water. In a large bowl mix together the flour and salt. Make a well in the middle of the flour, add the yeast, yoghurt and warm water and mix to a soft dough.

Turn on to a floured surface and knead until the dough is smooth and elastic. Prove the dough in a covered bowl in a warm place for 1–1½ hours, until doubled in size. (This first proving should be omitted if using easy-blend dried yeast.)

Divide the dough into two and knead lightly, working half the chopped walnuts with each piece of dough, and place into two 1½lb (680g) greased loaf tins. Cover with a clean tea towel and leave in a warm place until doubled in size.

Bake the loaves at 425°F/220°C/Gas 7 for 45 minutes. When cooked, the loaves should sound hollow when tapped. Turn out and cool on a wire rack.

CREDIT CRUNCH PIE

Clarrie says she can usually find the ingredients for this filling pie in the larder. Sometimes she adds some snipped pieces of bacon too. It makes a good, nourishing meal that costs very little.

FOR THE PASTRY

6oz (175g) plain wholemeal flour

2oz (55g) plain white flour

pinch of salt

2oz (55g) butter or hard margarine

2oz (55g) lard

2tbsp cold water

FOR THE FILLING

12oz (340g) potatoes

2 large onions

3tbsp vegetable oil

4oz (115g) mature, grated
  cheddar cheese

2tbsp single cream or milk

1tbsp chopped fresh parsley and chives

salt and pepper

Mix flours and salt in a bowl. Cut the fats into small pieces, then rub between the fingers until the mixture resembles fine breadcrumbs. Add the water and stir with a knife until the mixture gathers into a ball. Turn on to a floured board and knead slightly.

Grease a 9in (23cm) pie dish or flan tin. Roll out the pastry and line the dish.

To make the filling, boil the potatoes until tender. Chop the onions and sauté in the oil until soft. Mix the onions and potatoes together and add the cheese, cream, chopped parsley and chives and salt and pepper to taste.

Allow to cool, then fill the pastry case and dot with butter. Brush the edges of the pastry with water. Cover with a pastry lid and seal. Decorate with pastry leaves and prick the lid with a fork.

Bake in the centre of a hot oven at 425°F/220°C/Gas 7 for about 30 minutes until cooked through and golden on top.

UNCLE WALTER'S
WISDOM
Cure for a sore throat: 'Dip a
goose's feather in lard and rub it
on the back of yer throat.'

LAMB, LEEK AND PRUNE PIES

In Victorian times the hunting-lodges prepared traditional feasts for the gentry to enjoy in style and reasonable comfort. These savoury meat pies, served with hot soup, are most welcome on Brian's pheasant shoots.

FOR THE HOT WATER CRUST PASTRY
1lb (450g) plain flour
1tsp salt
7oz (200g) lard
7fl oz (200ml) water (approximately)

FOR THE FILLING
1tbsp sunflower oil
1 medium onion, finely chopped
1lb (450g) lamb, best neck fillet, trimmed and cubed
2 plump garlic cloves, finely chopped
3oz (85g) prunes, stoned and chopped
1 sprig fresh rosemary, chopped
1 leek, chopped
salt and pepper

To make the hot water crust pastry, sieve the flour and salt together in a bowl. Make a well in the centre. In a saucepan melt the lard in the water and bring to the boil, then pour into the well. Beat the mixture quickly to make a soft dough. Knead until a pliable dough is formed, adding a little extra flour if necessary. Leave covered for half an hour to allow the dough to become more elastic.

To make the pie filling, heat the oil in a large frying pan and fry the onion until translucent. Add the garlic and meat and fry until brown. Add the prunes and rosemary, cover and cook for 10 minutes. Finally, stir in the leek and seasoning and cook for a further 2–3 minutes. Spread the mixture on a plate and allow to cool.

Divide the pastry into 8 pieces and use two-thirds of each piece to line a 4in (10cm) individual quiche or Yorkshire pudding tin. Roll out the remaining third to form pastry lids.

Spoon the cooled meat mixture into the tins, moisten the edges of the pastry and press down the pastry lids. Brush the lids with oil and pierce a hole in the centre. Bake in a preheated oven at 350°F/180°C/Gas 4 for 30–40 minutes until brown.

VEGETABLE LASAGNE

Amy is keen to make this in the Vicarage kitchen. Aubergine adds an interesting 'meaty' texture. 'P'raps I can use one of those jars of pasta sauce you've got on the pantry shelf, to make it look a bit brighter', she said to Usha.

1 medium aubergine
4tbsp olive oil
1 large onion, chopped
1 garlic clove, crushed
1tbsp parsley, finely chopped
1tbsp fresh marjoram or oregano,
　chopped (or ¼tsp dried)
2 small courgettes, sliced
1 tin chopped tomatoes
4oz (115g) mushrooms, sliced
salt and pepper
6oz (175g) lasagne (the sort that doesn't
　need pre-cooking)

FOR THE SAUCE
2oz (55g) butter
2oz (55g) plain flour
20fl oz (1pt/600ml) milk
4oz (115g) grated cheese (Borsetshire
　or Cheddar)
2oz (55g) parmesan
black pepper and salt
grated nutmeg

Trim the ends off the aubergine but don't peel it. Cut into ½in (1cm) cubes.

Heat the oil in a large frying pan and cook the onion, garlic and herbs for 1 minute. Add the cubed aubergine and sliced courgettes and cook for a further 3–4 minutes, stirring occasionally. Add the tomatoes, mushrooms and seasoning, then cover and simmer for 20 minutes.

To make the sauce, put the butter, flour and milk into a saucepan and whisk over a moderate heat until the sauce has come to the boil and thickened. Add the grated cheese, nutmeg, salt and black pepper.

Assemble the lasagne by first putting a layer of the vegetable mixture in the bottom of an ovenproof dish, followed by a layer of lasagne sheets. Continue with alternate layers, ending with a layer of lasagne. Top this with the sauce and sprinkle with the finely grated parmesan.

Cover with foil and bake in a preheated oven at 400°F/200°C/Gas 6 for 40 minutes, removing the foil for the last 15 minutes.

SAVOURY SAUSAGE AND APPLE PLAIT

SERVES 4—5

This keeps well in the freezer and is ideal for a quick meal at home, or for a picnic. It is particularly good with Spicy September Chutney.

1 small onion, chopped
1 tbsp oil
2 sticks celery, washed and diced
1 small apple, peeled and chopped
1lb (450g) sausage meat
1 tsp ground thyme
salt and pepper
1 medium size egg, beaten
1½tsp mild curry powder
8oz (225g) puff pastry, home-made
** or frozen**

Fry the onion in the oil until soft and add the remaining ingredients. Stir well, and allow to cool a little.

Roll the pastry out into a rectangle, then spread the mixture down the centre of the pastry.

Brush the remaining edges of the pastry with beaten egg and make a series of diagonal cuts at ¼in (1cm) intervals down the longest sides of the rectangle. Starting at one end, fold the strips over, overlapping in the centre to form a plait. Continue until the filling is completely covered.

Paint the plaited top with beaten egg and bake in a preheated oven at 425°F/220°C/Gas 7 for 15 minutes. After this time, reduce the heat and cook for a further 20 minutes until the pastry is crisp and golden.

Serve either cold with the chutney or hot with braised red cabbage and a baked potato.

NOTES

Mabel Larkin used to boil her new rope clothes-line in the copper before using it, to prevent it from stretching and to make it last longer.

FRANKFURTERS WITH WARM POTATO SALAD

An easy Saturday lunch, little Ruairi's favourite. I think it reminds him of his early years in Germany with his mother. How sad!

Put 8 frankfurters into boiling water, remove from the heat and leave for 10 minutes.

1.8lb (675g) waxy new potatoes, scrubbed
4tbsp extra virgin olive oil
1tbsp white wine vinegar
3tbsp chopped chives
pepper and salt to taste

Boil the new potatoes in salted water until just tender. Toss in the olive oil and vinegar while still hot and add the chives. (If using small new potatoes they are better left unpeeled, but peel larger ones after boiling.)

If you prefer to serve this as a cold salad, mix 1tbsp mayonnaise with 2tbsp crème fraîche and turn the potatoes, when cold, into this creamy dressing.

Serve the frankfurters with the warm potato salad – so yummy with the beetroot purée and horseradish cream overleaf as well!

BEETROOT PURÉE

Beetroot is a vegetable which is undeservedly ignored. Perhaps it's the colour that proves off-putting. Here it's subtly earthy and unsubtly red.

1oz (25g) butter
1 large onion, finely chopped
1lb (450g) beetroot, cooked,
  peeled and chopped
1 plump garlic clove, crushed
2 medium cooking apples, peeled,
  cored and chopped
salt and pepper
½tsp powdered mace

Heat the butter and fry the onion over a low heat until transparent. Add the chopped beetroot, garlic, and apple and simmer over a low heat until amalgamated into a thick purée. Season with salt, freshly ground pepper and mace.

HOME-MADE HORSERADISH CREAM

Monday wouldn't be Monday without a good slice of cold sirloin, pink in the middle and spread with horseradish cream. 'Nobody cooked beef like my Pru', Uncle Tom used to tell me.

1lb (450g) horseradish
10fl oz (½pt/300ml) vinegar

Clean and scrub the horseradish roots thoroughly. Grate, either in a food processor or with a hand grater. (The horseradish will make your eyes smart and your fingers sore – this is a labour of love.)

Pack the grated horseradish into jars and cover with white wine vinegar.

To make the cream, mix some of the preserved horseradish with dried mustard powder, soured or double cream and a little sugar. It keeps for up to 2 weeks in a covered jar in the refrigerator.

Mix together freshly chopped, boiled beetroot with soured cream and horseradish sauce: excellent with cold meats.

COURGETTE CHEESE TART

Once again, an Ambridge favourite. The courgettes were from Bert using those confusing TEAS, Ambridge's own exchange system. This is a versatile tart which can be served cold with salad and parsleyed new potatoes, or hot straight from the oven, with its filling still puffy and light. I would be tempted to add some crushed garlic in with the courgettes for a little extra oomph.

FOR THE CHEESE PASTRY
6oz (175g) plain flour

½tsp salt

pinch cayenne pepper

pinch dry mustard

2oz (55g) butter or margarine

2oz (55g) finely grated good
   cheddar cheese

2tbsp cold water

FOR THE FILLING
12oz (340g) courgettes

1oz (25g) butter

1 medium chopped onion

¼tsp grated nutmeg

5fl oz (¼ pt/150ml) natural
   yoghurt or single cream

2 large size eggs or 3 smaller
   ones

2tbsp grated parmesan cheese

salt and pepper

Sift the flour, salt, pepper and mustard into a bowl. Rub in the butter until the mixture resembles fine breadcrumbs. Mix in the cheese and sprinkle on the cold water, then knead lightly to form a smooth dough, adding more water if necessary.

Roll out the pastry to line an 8in flan tin. Prick the base and bake blind at an oven temperature of 375°F/190°C/Gas 5 for 15–20 minutes, or until the pastry is just set.

To make the filling, wash the courgettes, cut off the stalks – but do not peel – and dice. Melt the butter, add the onion, courgettes and nutmeg and cook over a low heat until the courgettes are just tender. Leave to cool.

Beat the eggs, yoghurt, parmesan and seasoning together. Combine with the courgettes and pour into the pastry case. Bake for 300 minutes at 350°F/180°C/Gas 4.

Index tabs (left margin):

BAY LEAV

APPETIZERS	Tomato Juice Aspic
SOUPS	Vegetable Stock Herb Bouquet Fish Chowders
FISH	Pickled Fish Crab Shrimp
EGGS & CHEESE	
MEATS	Beef Veal Stews Lamb Pot Roast Boiled Ham Shish Kebab
POULTRY & GAME	Boiled Chicken Wild Game Fricassee Stews
VEGETABLES	Onions Boiled Potatoes Green Beans Carrots Eggplant Stewed Tomatoes
SALADS	Fish Aspic
SAUCES	All Marinades
DESSERTS & BEVERAGES	

BRIDGE FARM SATURDAY SAUSAGE BAKE

This is a whole meal in one pot. Pat is delighted when young Tom calls in and pops a couple of pounds of his best sausages into the fridge. I think I would use red wine instead of cider.

1tbsp oil
1lb (450g) thick pork sausages
6 rashers streaky bacon,
    cut into strips
2 leeks, sliced
2 onions, chopped
1tbsp flour
2 potatoes, thinly sliced
1 tin chopped tomatoes
2tbsp tomato purée
10fl oz (½pt/300ml) stock or cider
salt and pepper

Heat the oil in a flameproof casserole and fry the sausages. When browned, remove from the casserole, cut them through lengthways and reserve.

Add the bacon, leeks and onion and fry until the onion is soft. Add the flour and cook for a further 2–3 minutes.

Return the sausages to the casserole with the potatoes, tomatoes and tomato purée. Add the stock or cider and season.

Cover and bake in the oven at 375°F/190°C/Gas 5 for an hour, or until the potatoes are soft.

Lizzie Larkin used to polish her black kitchen range with a mixture of black boot polish, black lead and turpentine. Brushed on and then polished off, this kept the range brilliant for a month.

Autumn Jam

Makes about 5 lb.

2 lb. pears	
1 lb. plums or quinces	
1 pint water	
3 lb. sugar	

Peel and core or stone the fruit and cut into pieces.

Tie the peel and cores in a clean J-cloth or muslin. Place the fruit, bag and water in a large pan and simmer until fruit is completely tender. Remove bag and squeeze out juice. Make sure contents of the pan have been reduced by about half.

sugar has d
and boil rap
about 5 min
Pour into
waxed discs
label.

Blackb
for Di

Makes ab

1½ lb. coo
2 lb. black
Knob of b
¾ pint wa
3 tablesp
1 lb. fruc
3 Campd

Peel and
thinly.
Rub th
water in
Soften
minutes.
with a w
of the fr

CRUNCHY APPLE SALAD WITH HERB DRESSING

Quick and easy, this is a simple starter that is both satisfying and full of goodness. Adam likes this salad converted to a light lunchtime snack by the addition of flaked fillets of cold smoked mackerel or tuna. Garnish with lemon wedges and serve on a bed of salad leaves.

FOR THE HERB DRESSING

10oz (280g) natural yoghurt

3 spring onions, finely chopped

1tbsp snipped chives

1tbsp chopped fresh parsley

1tbsp chopped mint

½tsp curry powder

salt and freshly ground black pepper

4 dessert apples (Cox's Orange Pippins
  are ideal)

juice of 1 lemon

2oz (55g) chopped walnuts

2oz (55g) sultanas

1tbsp horseradish cream
  (see page 118)

First, make the dressing by mixing all those ingredients together. Thin with a little lemon juice if necessary. (Reserve a few chives for a garnish.)

For the salad, wash, core and chop the apples – but do not peel them. Toss in the lemon juice to prevent discolouration. Mix together with the chopped walnuts and sultanas, and then add the horseradish cream. Pile on to a bed of green salad and pour the herb dressing over. Decorate with a few snipped chives.

BATTERED PLUM BAKE

SERVES 4–6

Given to me by a French visitor, the original recipe uses black cherries but it can be made equally well with fresh plums. Tender young sticks of rhubarb sprinkled with ground ginger are delicious too.

1lb (450g) small sweet plums
6oz (175g) plain flour
pinch of salt
3 medium size eggs
3oz (85g) caster sugar
10fl oz (½pt/300ml) milk
a few drops almond essence
1tsp ground cinnamon
a little icing sugar

Cut the washed plums into halves or quarters depending on their size, and lay them skin side up on a greased baking dish.

Sieve the flour and salt into a bowl. Add the beaten eggs and sugar. Gradually stir in the milk and almond essence and beat until smooth. Pour the mixture over the plums and sprinkle with ground cinnamon.

Bake for 35–40 minutes at 350°F/180°C/Gas 4.

Dust with icing sugar before serving.

GOOD OLD-FASHIONED BREAD AND BUTTER PUDDING

SERVES 4

'We don't eat much bread, so this is a good way of using up the remainder of the loaf,' says Mum. 'Nice, this is,' said Jack, smacking his lips. 'Who's made it? Jean-Paul?'

6 thin slices of white bread, crusts removed
2oz (55g) butter
2tbsp marmalade
2oz (55g) currants
2 whole medium size eggs and 1 yolk
20fl oz (1pt/600ml) milk
grated zest of 1 lemon
2oz (55g) demerara sugar
1tsp cinnamon

Spread the bread slices with butter and marmalade and cut into triangles. Grease a 2pt (1.2l) pudding basin and arrange the bread in layers, sprinkling each layer with currants, and finishing with a layer of bread.

Beat the eggs and milk together, add the grated lemon zest and pour over the bread. Leave to stand for an hour.

Sprinkle the top of the pudding with the sugar and the cinnamon before baking in a preheated oven at 325°F/160°C/Gas 3 for 50–60 minutes. The top should be crusty and golden brown. Serve with cream or custard.

(If the eggs are separated and the whites folded in later, the pudding will be almost soufflé-like.)

Sprinkle sugar on custard to prevent a skin forming.

Apple Jelly

Makes about 1½ lb.

Windfall apples can be used for jelly so long as all bruised and damaged parts are cut out. Cooking apples or crab apples are also suitable — cooking apples make a golden jelly, crab apples a pink one.

2 lb. apples

1-1½ pints water

Juice of one lemon

5 whole cloves

Granulated sugar (see recipe)

Wash and cut up the apples including the core and skin. Place in a large pan with the water. there should be just

EVA'S APFELKUCHEN

Many years ago this apple cake was made by our au pair, Eva Lenz. I wonder what's happened to her now? And that policeman?

4oz (115g) butter
4oz (115g) caster sugar
8oz (225g) self-raising flour
1 medium size egg
1lb (450g) cooking apples
1tbsp brown sugar
1oz (25g) sultanas
1tsp cinnamon
a little icing sugar

Grease and line a loose-bottomed 8in (20cm) cake tin. Melt the butter in a saucepan over a low heat and add the sugar. Sift the flour into a bowl and combine with the beaten egg. Then stir in the butter and sugar mixture.

Peel, core and slice the apples. Put in a bowl and mix with the brown sugar, sultanas and cinnamon. Spread half the cake mixture in the bottom of the tin, arranging the spiced sugar and apple on top. Cover with the remaining cake mixture. (This is tricky and it doesn't matter if you leave gaps.)

Place the cake tin in a preheated oven at 350°F/180°C/Gas 4 and bake for about an hour or until golden.

Cool in the tin and either dust with icing sugar or drizzle over a thin icing glaze.

HUNGRY HUNTER'S CAKE (FOR DEBBIE) OR FAMISHED FARMER'S CAKE (FOR BRIAN)

Debbie used to say this was just the cake to be eaten after a healthy day's hunting or a day at the 'off-road' riding course. I'm not keen on Brian having too much cake these days. Don't be discouraged if it sinks in the middle.

12oz (340g) margarine
9oz (250g) demerara sugar
4 medium size eggs
grated zest and juice of 1 orange
2tbsp clear honey
15oz (420g) self-raising flour
2oz (55g) cocoa powder
1tsp mixed spice
8oz (225g) mixed peel
12oz (340g) seedless raisins

Cream together the margarine and sugar until soft.

Beat together the eggs, orange juice and honey, and gradually beat into the creamed mixture, with a little flour to prevent curdling. Fold in the rest of the sifted flour, cocoa, mixed spice and orange zest. Finally, stir in the mixed peel and raisins.

Place in a greased and lined 9in (23cm) cake tin. Cook at 325°F/160°C/Gas 3 for about 2–2½ hours, testing with a skewer (that should come away clean) to check it's cooked through. Cool in the tin before turning out on to a wire rack.

MAGRETS DE CANARD AUX CERISES

This was one of Jean-Paul's sweet and rather rich recipes in which the duck breasts are presented attractively in a pool of cherry sauce. The light fluffy rice makes a happy marriage. I think a sharp, palette-cleansing sorbet is called for after this.

4 large, boned duck breasts
3tbsp clear honey
1tbsp (175ml) lemon juice
6fl oz (170ml) dry white wine
11b (450g) morello cherries or 15oz (425g) can
  pitted cherries in syrup 2tsp sugar
1½tsp arrowroot
4tbsp cherry brandy or port
salt and pepper

Score the skin of the duck breast with a sharp knife. Blend the honey and lemon juice and spread over the skins, then leave to marinade for 30 minutes.

Place in a roasting tin, season and roast in the oven at 400°F/200°C/Gas 6 for about 30—40 minutes.

When cooked, take the duck breasts from the oven and transfer to a plate to keep warm. Skim any fat from the roasting pan, then place the pan over a high heat. Add the wine and stir with a wooden spoon to deglaze, reducing the liquid by half.

Remove the stones from the cherries, put the fruit to one side and add the cherry juice and sugar to the roasting pan, or the syrup from the canned cherries without extra sugar. Blend the arrowroot with the cherry brandy or port and pour into the boiling pan, stirring until the sauce thickens. Add the cherries and cook gently for 2—3 minutes.

Slice the duck breasts and arrange in an attractive fan shape on the plate, pouring a little sauce over them. Serve the duck with wild rice and pine nuts.

SORBET A L'ORANGE

Deliciously cooling and neither too tart nor too sweet.

6 sugar lumps
orange peel
9fl oz (250g) still mineral water
3½oz (90g) icing sugar
9fl oz (250ml) freshly squeezed
  orange juice
1tbsp lemon juice

Rub the orange peel with the lumps of sugar. The flavour will be absorbed into the sugar.

Put the mineral water, icing sugar and sugar lumps into a large bowl. Strain the freshly squeezed orange and lemon juice through a fine sieve and add to the mixture, stirring thoroughly.

Transfer to an ice cream maker and freeze. If you don't possess an ice cream maker, place in a freezer container and freeze for 2–3 hours, or until almost solid.

Remove from the freezer and beat thoroughly to break down the ice crystals. Return to the freezer for 1–2 hours until completely set.

Serve the sorbet scooped out in balls.

BLACKBERRY BUTTERSCOTCH CREAM

SERVES 4–6

This is based on a typical Danish dessert. Many years ago Bridge Farm's helping hand, Thorkil, suggested this superb recipe to Pat.

2 large cooking apples
1lb (450g) freshly picked blackberries
3tbsp clear honey
¼tsp cinnamon or half a cinnamon stick
5fl oz (¼pt/150ml) double cream
5fl oz (¼pt/150ml) yoghurt

FOR THE TOPPING
3oz (85g) unsalted butter
4oz (115g) coarse white breadcrumbs
1oz (25g) caster sugar

Peel and slice the apples and put with the rinsed blackberries in a saucepan. Add the honey and cinnamon, and simmer over a low heat until soft.

Remove the cinnamon stick, allow the fruit to cool a little and put into a glass bowl.

Whip the cream, adding the yoghurt spoonful by spoonful until thick. Keep to one side until the topping is made.

For the topping, melt the butter in a clean frying pan and add the breadcrumbs and sugar. Gently brown the breadcrumbs, stirring to prevent them from burning. When golden brown, spread out on to a large plate to cool.

Sprinkle some of these crunchy crumbs on to the fruit. Put the cream/yoghurt mixture on top and the remaining crumbs as a final layer.

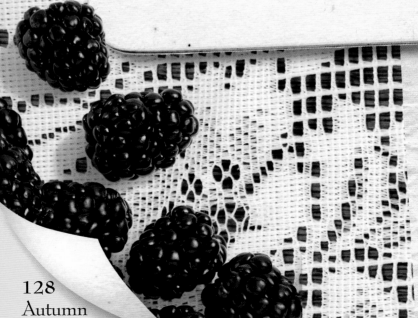

Add sugar. Stir over low heat until dissolved, then bring to the boil and boil rapidly until setting point is reached, about 5 minutes.
Pour into warm, clean jars, cover with waxed discs. Cover with lid or Cellophane while hot or cold.

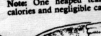

Apple and Ginger Jam

Makes about 2½ lb.

1½ lb. cooking apples, ready prepared
½ pint water
½ level teaspoon ground ginger
Grated rind and juice of 1 lemon
1½ lb. granulated sugar
1 oz. crystallised ginger

Peel, core and cut up the cooking apples. Tie the cores and skin in a new damp J-cloth or muslin and hang in the pan together with the

Fruit Salad Co

Makes 2-3 jars

2 lb. honeydew melon, from a 3½ lb. melon
1¼ lb. granulated sugar
2 small lemons
8 glacé cherries, quar

Cut the melon in half, into sections, then c away from the skin. Cu

MOCHA FUDGE SLICE

Rich, dark and irresistible but definitely not for those on a diet!

6oz (175g) soft margarine
4oz (115g) caster sugar
4 medium size eggs
2oz (55g) self-raising flour
6oz (175g) drinking chocolate
1tsp coffee granules, dissolved in
1tbsp hot water

FOR THE FUDGE TOPPING
3oz (85g) hard margarine
8oz (225g) icing sugar
2oz (55g) cocoa
2tbsp water

Cream the margarine and sugar together until light and fluffy and beat in the eggs one by one. Beat in the sifted flour and drinking chocolate and mix well. Add the dissolved coffee and beat thoroughly.

Spoon the mixture into two greased and lined 8in (20cm) sandwich tins, or one large one. Bake in a preheated moderate oven at 350°F/180°C/Gas 4 for about 20–25 minutes, until well risen and firm to the touch, and beginning to shrink away from the sides of the tins. Leave to cool in the tins.

To make the fudge topping, melt the margarine in a saucepan, add the sifted icing sugar and cocoa and cook for 1 minute, then beat until smooth and shiny.

Cool slightly, and then pour on to the cake, still in the tins. The fudge mixture will spread over the top of the cake and cool with a shiny surface.

Serve in slices with cream, ice-cream or yoghurt.

constantly towards the end of ... prevent sticking. Boil until thick.

Pour into warm, clean jars. Cover with waxed discs, waxed side down. Cover and label when cold.

What went wrong and why:
Mouldy jam: results from over-ripe fruit; slow or insufficient boiling with sugar; cold or damp jars; incorrect covering — the waxed discs should be put on when the jam is hot; poor storage.

Mould is not harmful but may affect the flavour — either scrape off and use jam immediately or remove the mould and boil jam up again. Repot in clean, warm jars and cover with waxed discs.

Jam does not set or a syrupy jam or jelly: results from lack of pectin (the fruit could have been over-ripe in which case the normal pectin has deteriorated); from insufficient boiling or over-boiling past setting point;

WINTER

It's as black as pitch, just a sparse sprinkling of stars and a moon as thin as a thumbnail, when poor Mike Tucker sets forth on the early morning milk round, wearing a jolly woolly cap, pulled down nearly to his nose, and finger-free knitted mittens. 'For my Granddad, to keep you warm this winter,' wrote a practical little Phoebe on her Christmas card. A feathering of fern-like frost patterns the panes of Willow Cottage and puddles in the yard are skimmed with a sheen of ice.

'My dear old Betty would be saying to me, "You stay in bed Mike, just a little bit longer. All folks have for breakfast now is a mouthful of apple or a munch on a crunchy cereal-bar on their way to work, if what I sells in my shop is anything to go by." But it's not, I know. Mr Pullen and the other old folk in Manorfield Close like hot milk on their porridge and a warm milky drink by their side. "Soothing posset, with honey", Mrs Blossom used to call it.'

The rime of frost has riveted Bridge Farm's root crop firmly to the solid Ambridge soil. Tony Archer's worried, furrowed brow frowns as he tucks into Tom's lightly grilled, home-reared savoury sausages, swilling them down with a mugful of strong sweet tea.

Meanwhile, up at Home Farm, Adam and Brian battle straw-deep amidst the noise and bleating in the warm lambing shed. New born twins totter on their tiny hooves to search for their instant milky comfort in this cold and cruel climate.

On the road out of Ambridge, Borchester-boutique-bound, advances a convoy of faux-fur clad females. Perched high and peering over steering wheels and hedges, this army of yummy-mummies sweeps grandly and effortlessly through highways and life, the seemingly sun-kissed Sabrinas and bonus-blessed Beesboroughs of this unbalanced world. High pitched and hands-free, voices piping single shrill snatches... 'chalets...snow...salopettes...prep-school place...nanny...the jolly Hunt Ball'.

Wafting with wintergreen and clutching a limp bunch of pale-berried mistletoe, old Mrs Potter leans and breathes heavily at the Post Office counter, a thin wad of grubby, thumbed notes and a couple of coins stuffed proudly into her flimsy purse. 'Off to have a mince pie with Mr Pullen now,' she chortles as she limps away.

A big, shiny, bombastically black vehicle backs smoothly down a manicured drive in Grange Spinney – the tailgate slides open and rattling crates are carried into the Thwaites' underfloor-heated, parqueted entrance hall, in readiness for a cosy, comfortably cosseted Christmas and a healthy, expectantly wealthy, New Year.

MISTY MEMORIES

DECEMBER

Over Sixties' Christmas Party

The glossy doors swung open and a wall of warmth greeted them, along with the clattering of crockery and conversation. Rubber heels and ferrules squeaked on waxed wooden floorboards,

while Marjorie Antrobus's remarkably unrheumatic fingers gave a jaunty rendition of Rudolf the Red-Nosed Reindeer. Stout trestles and indescribable undergarments creaked as ample bosoms and bottoms eased themselves into place. A curious haze of camphor and embrocation emanated from Joe in his Sunday-best corduroys. Steaming willow-patterned cups of tea were eagerly passed along the rows. There was a snapping of crackers and cracking of jokes and rather vulgar paper hats gluing themselves to glistening foreheads as Sid Perks struggled manfully into the moth-eaten garb of a steadily suffocating Father Christmas.

This was one of the wonderful Brookfield Christmases – logs crackling, crackers popping and Phil playing carols on the slightly out of tune piano. We ate too much and laughed so much.

LEMONY FORCEMEAT STUFFING

12oz (350g) white breadcrumbs
4tbsp chopped fresh herbs
  (marjoram, thyme, sage)
or 2tsp dried herbs
6tbsp chopped parsley
salt and pepper
grated zest and juice of 1 small
  lemon
6oz (175g) butter
3 medium size eggs

Mix together the breadcrumbs, herbs, chopped parsley, seasoning and grated lemon zest.

Melt the butter, mix the eggs and lemon juice and bind all the ingredients together to make a moist stuffing.

This is enough to stuff the breast of a 12–14lb (5.5–6.5kg) turkey.

CHESTNUT AND CELERY STUFFING

2lb (1kg) chestnuts
6 sticks celery
4oz (115g) soaked dried apricots
4oz (115g) white breadcrumbs
1tbsp chopped parsley
salt and freshly milled pepper
1 medium size egg
2oz (55g) melted butter

Slit the shells of the chestnuts, boil for 30 minutes, and shell while still hot. Press through a sieve.

Finely chop the celery and apricots. Combine with the breadcrumbs, parsley and seasoning and mix thoroughly with the beaten egg and melted butter.

This recipe is sufficient to stuff the cavity of a plucked and drawn 12lb (5.5kg) turkey.

CRUNCHY ROAST POTATOES

These are cooked in a separate roasting tin with 2 or 3oz (55–85g) melted cooking fat. First parboil the potatoes for 4–5 minutes. Drain, and then score the surface of the potatoes with a fork. For golden-brown, crisp potatoes, roast in the cooking fat in a roasting tin near the top of a hot oven 425°F/220°C/Gas 7 for about an hour, turning occasionally.

CRANBERRY AND ORANGE SAUCE

This can be put through a sieve or blender if a smoother sauce is preferred.

1lb (450g) fresh cranberries
5fl oz (¼pt/150ml) orange juice
1 cinnamon stick
6oz (175g) granulated sugar
grated zest of 1 orange

Put the cranberries in a saucepan with the orange juice and the cinnamon stick and bring slowly to the boil. Simmer gently. When the skins begin to pop, remove from the heat and stir in the sugar and the orange zest.

BRUSSELS SPROUTS WITH PINE NUTS

Prepare the sprouts by cutting off the outside leaves. Boil them in salted water in a lidded pan for 8–10 minutes, then drain well.

Place the pine nuts in a pan with melted butter and fry until brown. Pour the butter and nuts over the hot brussels sprouts and serve immediately.

CREAMED CELERIAC

SERVES 4–6

This is a smooth and creamy dish with a pronounced celery flavour. You may prefer freshly ground black pepper to the nutmeg or mace.

2lb (900kg) celeriac root
4oz (115g) unsalted butter
5fl oz (¼pt/150ml) double cream
2tsp caster sugar
½tsp grated nutmeg or mace

Peel the celeriac, cut into large chunks and place in a saucepan. Boil in salted water until tender. Drain well, then return to the pan to dry over a very low heat. Mash thoroughly, or purée in a blender or food processor.

Melt the butter in a pan over a low heat, add the celeriac, cream, sugar and seasoning. Keep stirring until the purée is well mixed and piping hot.

BRANDY BUTTER

6oz (175g) unsalted butter
8oz (225g) icing sugar
zest of 1 small orange
2tbsp brandy

Sift the icing sugar and cream with the butter. Add the orange zest, and then beat in the brandy. Chill before serving.

Jill makes on easy sweet sauce for puddings by mixing together, over a low heat, the juice and grated zest of an orange and a lemon, ½ teacup of runny honey and a beaten egg, stirring till it thickens.

CHRISTMAS PUDDING

Jill Archer's special rich Christmas pudding recipe, handed down from the Forrest family, has been added to and improved by Jill over the years. Remember to heat the brandy or rum in a warm spoon before pouring it over the pudding and lighting it. 'Watch out for the silver sixpence and be careful of your crown, Phil!'

4 dessert apples, peeled and finely chopped
8oz (225g) sultanas
8oz (225g) raisins
8oz (225g) currants
2oz (55g) chopped mixed peel
2oz (55g) glacé cherries
6½fl oz (185ml) dark rum
8oz (225g) self-raising flour
1oz (25g) ground ginger
1tsp mixed spice
8oz (225g) shredded suet
4oz (115g) soft brown sugar
2oz (55g) ground almonds
1oz (25g) flaked almonds
14oz (400g) fresh white breadcrumbs
2 medium size eggs
juice of 1 orange
juice of 1 lemon
30fl oz (900ml/1½ pt) (approximately) old ale

Assemble all the fruit in a large bowl and soak generously in rum. Leave in a cool place overnight, covered with a cloth.

Sieve the flour and spices together and add the suet, sugar, ground and flaked almonds and breadcrumbs. Mix into the fruit.

Beat the eggs in a separate basin, together with the fruit juices and remaining rum before adding to the fruit mixture. Finally add the ale, mixing thoroughly to obtain a 'loose batter' consistency. Cover with a cloth and leave overnight.

The next day divide the mixture into two basins, cover with a double thickness of greaseproof paper and steam for up to 10 hours. The longer the steaming the darker the puddings will be. Remember to keep topping up the water. Cool and replace the covers.

On Christmas Day, steam briskly for 2 hours and then serve with brandy butter.

CHOCOLATE YULETIDE LOG

SERVES 6–8

Some grumble that this is not a conventional Christmas cake, but there's no fear of raisin seeds finding their way under Jack's dentures with this deliciously rich recipe!

3 large size eggs
4oz (115g) caster sugar
3oz (85g) plain flour
1oz (25g) cocoa
1tbsp hot water

FOR THE CHOCOLATE BUTTER CREAM
4oz (115g) butter
8oz (225g) icing sugar
4oz (115g) plain dark chocolate (melted)
2tbsp strong black coffee

Grease and line a 12 x 9in (30 x 23cm) Swiss roll tin.

Whisk the eggs and sugar in a bowl with an electric hand whisk, over a pan of hot water, until pale and creamy. Sift in the flour and cocoa, folding in with a metal spoon. Gently stir in the hot water.

Pour into the prepared tin and bake in a preheated oven at 400°F/200°C/Gas 6 for approximately 10 minutes, or until the cake feels springy when lightly pressed.

Turn the cake out on to greaseproof paper and roll it up with a layer of well-sugared greaseproof paper inside. Allow to cool.

To make the chocolate butter cream, beat the softened butter with the sifted icing sugar until fluffy, then thoroughly stir in the melted chocolate and coffee.

When the cake is cold, gently remove the paper and spread the cake with a little of the chocolate butter cream. Reroll it and decorate with the remaining cream, using a fork to make the tree bark markings. Dust with icing sugar and decorate with a Christmas robin.

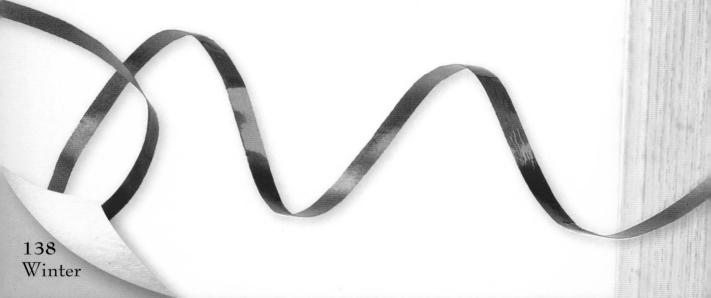

CHUNKY CHRISTMAS CRUNCH

SERVES 6 AT LEAST

A wickedly rich concoction for chocolate lovers, even more so when served with cream. Children often prefer this to a real fruity Christmas pud.

8oz (225g) butter
2tbsp golden syrup
8oz (225g) good quality
  dark chocolate
1tbsp cocoa powder
1tbsp dark rum
8oz (225g) plain sweet biscuits,
  crushed
6oz (175g) Uncle Walter's
  ginger nuts (see page 168),
  crushed
2oz (55g) preserved ginger,
  chopped
2oz (55g) glacé cherries,
  halved
2oz (55g) walnut pieces,
  chopped
a sprig of holly

Melt the butter, syrup and chocolate in a saucepan over a low heat. Stir in the cocoa and rum, then add the crushed biscuits, ginger pieces, cherries and chopped walnuts.

Spoon the mixture into a greased 2pt (1.2l) pudding basin, pressing down well.

Chill in a fridge to harden, dipping the basin in hot water before turning out. Decorate with a colourful sprig of holly.

JILL'S LEMON BOODLES FOOL

Very simple and quickly made, this is a light, tangy and refreshing alternative to the rich Christmas puddings.

24 boudoir sponge fingers
10fl oz (½ pt/300ml) double cream
10fl oz (½ pt/300ml) Greek yoghurt
juice and grated zest of 4 oranges
  and 2 lemons
2tbsp caster sugar

Crumble twelve of the sponge fingers into the base of a glass bowl.

Put the cream into a large mixing bowl with the grated orange and lemon zest. Squeeze the juice from the fruit, sieve it and stir in the sugar until dissolved.

Whip the cream and the yoghurt together, slowly adding the fruit juice.

Pour half of this whipped cream mixture on to the sponge fingers, add the remaining crumbled sponge fingers and top with the rest of the cream. Chill in the fridge for several hours before serving.

A little finely grated lemon zest to garnish adds an extra zing.

BRANDY WAFERS

Jill usually offers these to accompany her Lemon Boodles Fool. She sometimes makes little brandy wafer baskets. Instead of rolling up the warm biscuits, she shapes them by carefully placing them into tiny coffee cups, then removing them when they've cooled.

4oz (115g) butter
4oz (115g) demerara sugar
4oz (115g) golden syrup
2tsp brandy
4oz (115g) plain flour
1tsp (level) ground ginger
1tsp (level) cinnamon

In a saucepan warm the butter, sugar and syrup together gently on a low heat. When the butter has melted add the brandy. Sift in the flour, together with the cinnamon and ground ginger and mix well.

Drop teaspoonfuls of the mixture on to a greased baking tray, leaving plenty of room for them to spread. Bake for 10 minutes at 350°F/180°C/Gas 4.

Leave to cool for a minute then roll up each biscuit around the handle of a wooden spoon. Cool on a wire tray.

MINCE PIES MAKES 16 PIES

This pastry recipe, also Jill's, makes the mince pies crumbly and deliciously moreish. Heat them again before serving and to make them even more special, a dollop of cream cheese mixed with grated orange zest can be popped under each pastry lid.

8oz (225g) plain flour
pinch of salt
5oz (140g) butter
2oz (55g) ground almonds
4oz (115g) caster sugar
grated zest of half a lemon
1 medium size egg beaten
1lb (450g) Jill's special mincemeat

Sieve together the flour and salt and rub in the butter until it resembles fine breadcrumbs. Stir in the ground almonds, sugar and lemon zest and bind together with the beaten egg. Chill for 30 minutes before using.

Roll the pastry out to ¼ in (5mm) thick, and cut out bases and lids to fit greased patty tins. Place 1tsp of mincemeat in each base, and top with a dampened pastry lid. Prick each pie with a fork and bake for 25–30 minutes near the top of a hot oven at 400°/200°/Gas 6 until golden brown.

MINCEMEAT

MAKES ABOUT 5LB/2.25KG

There's a bit of an argument as to whether this is Doris's recipe or Auntie Pru's, but it's jolly good whoever first made it!

1lb (450g) cooking apples
4oz (115g) candied peel
4oz (115g) blanched almonds
8oz (225g) dried apricots
1lb (450g) shredded suet
8oz (225g) stoned raisins
8oz (225g) sultanas
4oz (115g) chopped glacé cherries
1lb (450g) soft brown sugar
1tsp cinnamon
10fl oz (½pt/300ml) ginger wine
1 small wine glass brandy
grated zest and juice of 2 lemons

Peel, core and chop the apples. Chop the peel, nuts and dried apricots. Place these and all the remaining ingredients in a large bowl, and mix well.

The mincemeat can be stored in an earthenware jar with a well-fitting lid, or put into individual covered jars. Use within one month.

MULLED WINE

When the carol singers arrive from St Stephen's, on a cold and frosty evening just before Christmas, they will certainly be welcomed with mulled wine and mince pies.

6oz (175g) caster sugar
13fl oz (375ml) water (or half 75cl bottle)
55fl oz (2¾pt/1.5l) red wine (or 2 x 75cl bottles)
1 lemon, stuck with 6 cloves
1 inch piece of fresh root ginger thinly pared
zest of 1 orange
1 cinnamon stick
juice of 2 lemons

Measure the sugar and water into a saucepan and stir over a low heat until the sugar has dissolved. Add the wine and the rest of the ingredients and heat gently until steaming.

Remove from the heat, cover and allow to stand for 10 minutes. Remove the cinnamon, lemon, ginger and cloves, but leave the orange zest to float in the wine. Pour into a warmed punch bowl.

For red wine stains splash with soda water or white

CHOCOLATE CHERRY FUDGE

Alice used to help me make this when she was a little girl. She particularly liked licking out the bowl! Chopped nuts can be used instead of cherries if you prefer.

4oz (115g) plain chocolate
4oz (115g) butter
3tbsp milk
1lb (450g) icing sugar, sifted
½tsp vanilla essence
4oz (115g) glacé cherries, chopped

Melt the chocolate and butter in a heavy saucepan over a low heat. Add the milk gradually, stirring all the time. Add the sifted icing sugar and boil gently until the mixture thickens.

Remove from the heat, add the vanilla flavouring and beat until the mixture becomes thick and creamy. Stir in the glacé cherries.

Pour into a buttered 8 x 6in (20 x 15cm) tin and lightly mark into squares. Leave in the refrigerator for 1–2 hours until set, then cut into squares and store in an airtight container for 2–3 weeks.

PEPPERMINT CREAMS

Manorfield Close is engulfed in peppermint creams at Christmas time. Good for the digestion! I think this is Mrs Potter's old recipe.

1 medium size egg white
8oz (225g) icing sugar
1tsp peppermint essence
a few drops of green food colouring

In a bowl, beat the egg white until stiff. Add the sifted icing sugar. Beat in the peppermint essence until the mixture is a stiff, smooth paste, then drop in the green colouring and mix again.

Roll out on a board sprinkled with icing sugar. Cut out into rounds with a very small pastry cutter. Leave to set hard for 24 hours.

MISTY MEMORIES

JANUARY

Home Farm

Frosty, crisp days found the girls smart in their hacking-jackets on brisk country rides, their soft-muzzled ponies trotting down tree-lined bridleways, through Leaders Wood and Lyttleton Cover, and along by the side of our trout-rich lake. Alice and I went winter walking, making the most of nature's bounty, picking armfuls of berried branches and trailing evergreens, returning home before the fast-fading twilight.

HOME FARM VENISON AND PHEASANT CASSEROLE

This rich casserole is a delectable combination of our home produce and a wonderful way to entice new customers. It is on the menu when Brian invites members of the shoot or Borchester Land to dinner.

**2lb (1kg) haunch of venison, sliced
and cut into bite-size cubes
3 pheasant breasts,
sliced into slivers
2 large onions, chopped
1 plump garlic clove, crushed
sprig of fresh sage, chopped
1tsp honey mustard
26fl oz (750ml) red wine
(or 1 x 75cl bottle)
olive oil for frying**

FOR THE MARINADE
**3tbsp olive oil
4 garlic cloves, crushed
2tbsp juniper berries, crushed
zest and juice of 2 oranges
salt and pepper**

Mix together all the ingredients for the marinade, adding half the bottle of red wine, place in two covered bowls and marinate the venison and pheasant separately overnight. Remove the venison and pheasant from the marinade, pat dry on absorbent kitchen roll and keep separate. Strain and reserve the marinade.

In a large frying pan heat 1tbsp of olive oil and quickly fry the venison until browned on all sides. Remove to an ovenproof casserole.

Fry the pheasant breast slices in the pan over a fairly high heat until just browned on both sides, then remove to a separate dish. Add a little more oil to the pan and fry the onions and garlic for about a minute. Transfer to the casserole containing the venison.

Add the sage, the remainder of the bottle of wine and the reserved marinade to the casserole. Stir in the honey mustard and season.

Place in a moderate oven at 325°F/160°C/Gas 3 and cook for 1 hour, then add the pheasant breast. Continue cooking for another hour, or until the meat is tender.

Pour the casserole juices into a saucepan, skim off the fat and boil briskly to thicken the sauce. Pour over the meat, cover and keep warm until ready to serve with roast parsnips, parboiled and baked in cooking oil and butter for 45 minutes at 375°F/190°C/Gas 5, until brown all over.

GLAZED PARSNIPS AND CARROTS

SERVES 6

Ideal with any roast meat, these are particularly good with beef and Yorkshire pudding. Add sweet potatoes and some red onions for a delicious mélange.

1lb (450g) carrots
1lb (450g) parsnips
pinch of salt
2oz (55g) butter
grated zest and juice of 1 orange
½oz (15g) caster sugar
chopped parsley to garnish

Peel and slice the carrots thinly. Peel and quarter the parsnips, cutting out the woody centres before slicing them thickly. Put the vegetables in a pan, covering with water, add the salt and boil until barely tender.

Drain, then add the butter, orange zest and juice and sugar to the vegetables in the pan.

Cook steadily at first, then more vigorously, shaking the pan. The juice will reduce and form a glaze. Serve sprinkled with chopped parsley.

BAKED GARLIC POTATOES

This is a favourite way of cooking baked potatoes at Home Farm. Simple and scrumptious. Don't forget the crunchy sea salt.

Choose potatoes weighing about 3oz (85g) each. Scrub the skins thoroughly and rub liberally with olive oil and sea salt. Place in a large ovenproof casserole, preferably earthenware, and scatter at least a dozen unpeeled garlic cloves into the casserole. Drizzle in a little extra oil, replace the lid and bake for about 1¼ hours at 350°F/180°C/Gas 4. The cooked garlic cloves, with their creamy centres, can be served with the potatoes.

TRAWLERMAN'S PIE

Kathy used to cook this at The Bull. She sometimes added a layer of quartered hard-boiled eggs before spreading the potato over the top. The cheese can be mixed together with the creamy mashed potato if preferred. Not quite as up-market as Lilian's posh recipe! (see page 22)

1½lb (675g) cod fillet
15fl oz (¾pt/425ml) milk
1½oz (40g) butter
1 small onion, chopped
2tbsp chopped celery
1½oz (40g) flour
4oz (115g) mushrooms, sliced
2tbsp chopped parsley
2tsp anchovy essence
salt and pepper
5fl oz (150ml/¼pt) single cream
1lb (450g) potatoes, boiled and
    mashed
3oz (85g) grated cheese

Put the fish in a saucepan, cover with the milk and poach for 10 minutes. When cooked, take out the fish and flake it, removing any skin and bones, and reserve the cooking liquid.

Heat the butter in a saucepan, add the chopped onion and celery and fry until tender. Blend in the flour and stir to make a roux. Slowly add the reserved milk, stirring thoroughly, to make a smooth sauce. Bring to the boil and simmer for 2 minutes.

Add the sliced mushrooms, chopped parsley, anchovy essence, seasoning and cream. Add the flaked fish to the sauce and pour into an ovenproof dish. Cover with the mashed potato and sprinkle with grated cheese.

Bake in a preheated oven at 375°F/190°C/Gas 5 for about 20 minutes, until the top is golden.

Jill says, 'Carrots and dried apricots, boiled together then puréed and seasoned with mace, make a good smooth sauce to accompany roast loin of pork.'

BRAISED RED CABBAGE WITH APPLES

The smell of this piquant dish simmering on the Aga always makes me think of Christmas. The amount of sugar and vinegar can be adjusted to your liking. Pop in a cinnamon stick to add to the flavour and a few cranberries too, if you have some, for the sauce.

1tbsp vegetable oil
1 large onion, chopped
1 medium head of red cabbage
  (about 1½lb/650g)
2 large cooking apples
salt and black pepper
2tbsp demerara sugar
5tbsp red wine vinegar
a little water
salt and pepper

Heat the oil in a large saucepan and cook the onion until soft.

Shred the cabbage, cutting away the core.

Peel, core and slice the apples and add these and the cabbage to the onion. Add the rest of the ingredients, with just enough water to prevent the cabbage sticking to the bottom of the pan.

Cover with a lid and simmer gently for about 1–1½ hours.

NOTES

AUNTIE PRU'S RECIPE FOR PICKLING VINEGAR

Add a stick of cinnamon, a few red chillies, whole cloves, black peppercorns, mace and allspice berries to the vinegar while heating. Bring to the boil, then cool, strain and bottle.

STEAK, KIDNEY AND MUSHROOM PUDDING

SERVES 4–6

Ian kindly made this for Jack from Mum's old recipe. 'Ooh, Peggy, I like this! Why haven't you made this before?' Jack always enthuses as he licks his lips.

1lb (450g) best stewing steak, trimmed of excess fat
4oz (115g) lamb's kidney, skinned, cored and cubed
2tbsp flour
salt and pepper
3tbsp oil
1 large onion, chopped
6oz (175g) button mushrooms, thickly sliced
3 pickled walnuts, diced
6fl oz (175ml) beef stock

FOR THE SUET CRUST PASTRY
8oz (225g) plain or self-raising flour
½tsp salt
½tsp baking powder
3oz (85g) shredded suet
1tbsp horseradish sauce
about 4fl oz (125ml) water

To make the filling, cut the steak into 1 in (2.5cm) cubes. Toss the steak and kidney in the flour and season with salt and pepper. Heat the oil in a frying pan and add the meat to the pan, frying in small batches. When browned, remove to a casserole dish.

Fry the onion until lightly brown and transfer to the casserole, adding the mushrooms, walnuts and stock. Cover the casserole and simmer on a low heat or in a low oven (325°F/160°C/Gas 3) for an hour. Allow to cool.

To make the pastry, sieve the flour, salt and baking powder into a bowl. Stir in the suet and the horseradish sauce and mix to a soft dough with cold water.

Turn on to a floured board and knead until smooth. Roll out two-thirds of the dough and line a 2pt (1.2l) pudding basin.

Spoon the meat and gravy into the suet-lined basin. Roll out a pastry lid from the remains of the suet crust, moisten the edges and press firmly down to seal. Cover with a lid of greaseproof paper and foil, both pleated to allow room for the crust to rise. Steam or boil steadily for 2½–3 hours, remembering to top up the water level from time to time.

BUTTERED CARAWAY CABBAGE

SERVES 4—6

As a child I just did not like caraway seeds but Ruairi does. Maybe he acquired a taste for them when he lived in Germany with his mother.

1½lb (675g) white cabbage
5fl oz (¼pt/150ml) salted water
bay leaf
2oz (55g) butter
1tsp caraway seeds
salt and black pepper

Shred the cabbage finely and steam or boil in the salted water with the bay leaf, until cooked but still quite crisp. Drain and discard the bay leaf.

Melt the butter in the pan, add the cabbage and reheat. Sprinkle on the caraway seeds and freshly ground black pepper, tossing the mixture with a spaghetti fork. Serve at once.

WINTER SALAD WITH YOGHURT DRESSING

SERVES 8–10 AS A
SIDE SALAD

This crisp salad with its smooth dressing makes a fine accompaniment to roast ham.

FOR THE SALAD
1 small white cabbage, finely shredded
½ head celery, trimmed and sliced
4oz (115g) chopped walnut pieces
2 leeks, the white part cleaned and finely sliced
8oz (225g) carrots, grated

FOR THE YOGHURT DRESSING
5oz (140g) natural yoghurt
1tbsp olive oil
2tsp cider, wine vinegar or lemon juice
1tsp wholegrain or Dijon mustard
salt and pepper

To make the salad, combine all the ingredients.

To make the dressing, mix all the ingredients together thoroughly. Add chopped fresh parsley or chives if preferred, and season to taste. Pour this dressing over the salad and serve.

CLARET JELLY WITH SWEET SYLLABUB

The clever combination of flavours and textures makes this heady dessert a triumph.

FOR THE CLARET JELLY
8oz (225g) caster sugar
8fl oz (225ml/½pt) hot water
1fl oz (30ml) blackcurrant syrup
1oz (25g) gelatine
1tbsp brandy
20fl oz (1pt/600ml) claret

FOR THE SWEET SYLLABUB
1 lemon
10fl oz (½pt/300ml) white wine
1tbsp brandy
3oz (85g) caster sugar
20fl oz (1pt/600ml) double cream

To make the claret jelly, dissolve the sugar in 6fl oz (175ml) of water in a saucepan over a low heat. Stir in the blackcurrant syrup.

Sprinkle the gelatine into the remaining 2fl oz (50ml) of water, and dissolve in a bowl over a pan of hot water. Stir until dissolved.

Stir the dissolved gelatine into the blackcurrant mixture and then add the claret and brandy.

Pour into glasses and chill until set.

To make the syllabub, pare the zest thinly from the lemon and squeeze out the juice. Place the lemon zest, juice, white wine and brandy in a large bowl and leave overnight.

Strain, then add the sugar and stir until dissolved.

Whip the double cream into the wine, bringing it up into soft peaks, then chill.

Top each glass of claret jelly with a swirl of syllabub and serve.

GINGER TIPSY TRIFLE

This should serve 10 people, or 8 greedy ones! It's lucky we had a slimming club in Ambridge.

FOR THE BASE
1 fatless ginger sponge (or
a packet of fatless sponge
cakes)
1lb (450g) ginger marmalade
¼ bottle ginger wine
(approximately 2 wine
glasses)
20fl oz (1pt/600ml)
home-made Rich Custard
Cream or a packet variety

FOR THE TOPPING
20fl oz (600m/1pt) double
cream
2oz (55g) split blanched
almonds
2oz (55g) crystallized ginger

For the fatless ginger sponge, follow the same recipe as the Chocolate Yuletide Log (see page 138), substituting 1tsp ground ginger for the chocolate. Bake either in two 7 in (18cm) sponge cake tins or in a Swiss roll tin. Cool flat on a wire tray and cut into 1 in (2.5cm) fingers.

Split the sponge cake fingers and sandwich with the ginger marmalade. Place at the bottom of a glass bowl. Pour the ginger wine over the sponge and cover with a layer of the custard, then chill.

To make the topping, whip the cream until it stands in peaks and spread a thick layer over the custard. Decorate with split, blanched almonds and crystallized ginger.

Invitation

Sabrina and Richard Thwaite wish to
invite you to Grange Spinney for a
fish supper and a glass of fizz.

TREACLE, LEMON AND GINGER TART

SERVES 4–6

*A typical English pudding. Mum baked this for her American friend, Conn.
'Better than pecan pie', he told her.*

6oz (175g) plain flour
½tsp ground ginger
pinch of salt
3oz (85g) butter or hard margarine
cold water to mix
2oz (55g) fresh white breadcrumbs
½tsp ground ginger
juice of half a lemon
8oz (225g) golden syrup
grated zest of 1 lemon
1tbsp demerara sugar

Sift the flour, ½tsp of ginger and salt into a bowl. Rub in the butter until it resembles fine breadcrumbs. Add the cold water to mix to a stiff dough and knead until smooth. Wrap in foil and chill in the fridge for half an hour.

Roll the pastry out on a floured surface and line an 8 in (20cm) fluted flan dish. Reserve the pastry trimmings.

Prick the base of the tart and sprinkle on the breadcrumbs, ½tsp of ground ginger and lemon zest. Pour on the syrup and lemon juice – the syrup will spread itself over the crumbs. Sprinkle with demerara sugar and decorate the top with a lattice of pastry strips.

Bake in a moderately hot oven at 400°F/200°C/Gas 6 for 25 minutes or until the pastry is golden.

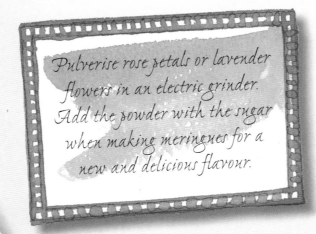

Pulverise rose petals or lavender flowers in an electric grinder. Add the powder with the sugar when making meringues for a new and delicious flavour.

BOMBE SURPRISE WITH APRICOT SAUCE AND ALMOND PRALINE

SERVES 4–6

Brian says this tastes much better than it looks, hence the name. If you don't have the time or the patience to make the meringues, bought ones will work equally well. Break them into pieces and pop them briefly under a hot grill to brown.

3 medium egg whites
6oz (175g) caster sugar
15fl oz (¾pt/425ml) double cream
2oz (55g) dried no-soak apricots
3tbsp almond liqueur (amaretto)
1tbsp (heaped) sifted icing sugar

To make the meringues, whisk the egg whites until stiff, gradually whisking in half of the caster sugar, folding in the remainder with a spatula or a metal spoon. Spoon the meringue into heaps on to an oiled baking sheet. Bake in a very low oven at 200°F/100°C for about 2 hours, leaving in the switched off oven to cool and dry out. Remove from the baking sheet and break into small pieces.

Whip the cream until fairly stiff, forming light peaks.

Chop the apricots finely. Fold the apricots, liqueur, icing sugar and meringue into the cream.

Lightly oil a bombe mould, or line with cling film. (Alternatively, you can use a 2¼ pt (1.3l) pudding basin.) Spoon in the creamy mixture, cover with foil and freeze for at least 5 hours.

To serve, dip the mould/basin briefly into a sink of hot water and turn out on to a plate. Leave for 8–10 minutes.

To make the apricot sauce, pour hot water over 8oz (225g) apricots and soak for 1 hour. Drain and place in a pan with 1oz (25g) caster sugar, the juice of 1 lemon and 10fl oz (½pt/300ml) water. Bring to the boil and simmer until soft, then sieve or blend in a food processor. Pour back into the rinsed pan, add the amaretto if desired, and heat gently. The sauce can also be served cold.

To make the almond praline, heat 4oz (115g) caster sugar and 2tbsp water in a thick-bottomed saucepan, and boil gently without stirring until it becomes a thick, golden-brown syrup. Remove from the heat and stir in the almonds. Grease a board with butter and pour on the mixture; cool, then crush with a rolling pin. Sprinkle on the bombe before serving. The praline should be stored in an airtight tin.

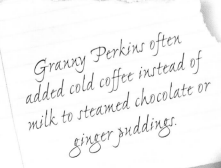

Granny Perkins often added cold coffee instead of milk to steamed chocolate or ginger puddings.

MISTY MEMORIES

FEBRUARY

Shrove Tuesday

Orders for the expedition to watch the Shrove Tuesday Pancake Race at Penny Hassett were issued by Marjorie Antrobus.

Number 4 platoon is to leave Manorfield Close at 10.45 precisely.

'Company, march!'

Dressed not in regulation pinafore-style battledress nor carrying steel frying pans, but clad wisely in well-worn overcoats, pac-a-macs and plastic hoods. Bowed backs battled against the wind. Flailing umbrellas fought the driving rain. 'February fill-dyke — what did I tell yer? You mark my words, they'll call it off.' Uncle Tom's voice, full of doom and gloom.

'Company, advance!' Leaving behind the pounding feet of pancake-tossing Penny Hassett housewives. Swinging the snug doors shut against the elements. Shaking off the beaded droplets. Stamping their feet and sinking onto cushioned settles in the comfort of The Griffin's Ploughman's Bar to the final command, 'Company, (thankfully) HALT!'

PANCAKES

This is Jill Archer's traditional pancake recipe.
Choose a small omelette or frying pan with a heavy base and make sure the oil is really hot. The edges of the pancake should be brown and crispy.

4oz (115g) plain flour
pinch salt
1 medium size egg and
** 1 egg yolk**
10fl oz (½pt/300ml) milk
1tbsp cooking oil or
** melted butter**

Sift the flour and salt into a mixing bowl. Make a well in the centre and drop in the egg and the extra yolk. Gradually beat or whisk in the milk until the batter is smooth and not lumpy. Leave the batter to rest for 30 minutes, then add the oil and give another whisk. (It should have the consistency of cream.)

Heat the pan until it is really hot, swirl some oil around to coat the base, and pour off any excess.
Add about 2tbsp of batter to the pan and swirl it around evenly. Cook for about a minute until the underside is golden, then turn or toss it and brown the other side.
The pancakes can either be folded in half and half again, or stacked one on top of the other, and kept warm in a buttered ovenproof dish, covered in foil, in a low oven.
Traditional pancakes are served drenched in lemon juice and sprinkled with sugar.

PARGETTER PANCAKES

MAKES 8

Nigel learnt the art of making pancakes from Jill Archer, or so he says, and tossing them too. I think Elizabeth makes this up-market version for lunch. Use buckwheat flour if possible, to make them closer to Russian blinis.

4fl oz (125ml) thick sour cream (or double cream with added lemon juice)
4oz (115g) smoked salmon, sliced
1 small jar lumpfish roe

Make the pancakes as before then, while hot, spread them with soured cream, laying on slices of smoked salmon.

Roll the pancakes up, topping each with a dollop of cream and a scattering of caviar.

JEAN-PAUL'S CRÊPES AUX POMMES

SERVES 4–6

I have given this recipe to Ian. He says he prefers to use Cox's Orange Pippins.

4 large dessert apples
2oz (55g) butter
4oz (115g) soft brown sugar
juice and grated zest of 1 orange

Peel, core and slice the apples.

Melt the butter in a heavy saucepan and add the apples, sugar, orange juice and zest. Cook until the apples are soft.

Make the pancakes as described before, and lay them in a dish, stacked one above the other, sandwiching with the apple mixture.

Cover with foil and reheat in a moderate oven 350°F/180°C/Gas 4 for 10 minutes.

Cut into wedges and serve with cream.

LIZZIE LARKIN'S COUNTRY LOAF

This recipe, which should be enough for two loaves, is quick and simple to make and requires no yeast. It freezes well too. Old Jethro would have polished these off in no time.

8oz (225g) wholewheat flour
8oz (225g) plain flour
2tsp cream of tartar
1tsp (level) salt
1tsp bicarbonate of soda
1tsp sugar 2oz (55g) margarine or lard
10fl oz (½pt/300ml) sour milk or
 buttermilk

Grease and flour a baking tray. Sift the dry ingredients twice. Rub in the lard and mix to a loose dough with the milk, adding a little at a time. Knead the dough lightly on a surface sprinkled with brown flour.

Shape into two loaves, leave for 10 minutes and then bake at 375°F/190°C/ Gas 5 for 30 minutes. Eat while very fresh.

THREE-FRUIT HONEY MARMALADE

This is Jill Archer's recipe using some of her own honey. 'Sunshine in a jar' old Bert calls it. You can make it at any time of the year and can use muscovado sugar for a darker marmalade, although you will achieve a softer set.

3 grapefruits
3 sweet oranges
3 lemons
3lb (1.5kg) clear honey
80fl oz (2.3l/4pt) water

Wash and dry the fruit. Squeeze the juice, remove the flesh and pips and tie them in a muslin bag. Place the juice and bag in a preserving pan, and add the finely sliced peel.

Add the water, bring to the boil and simmer for about 2 hours.

Remove the muslin bag. Stir in the honey until it has dissolved and then boil rapidly until set. Pull the preserving pan to one side off the heat when testing for setting point – this marmalade can overcook very easily.

Skim, leave to cool for 30–45 minutes, then pour into warmed jars to seal and label.

MRS BAGSHAWE'S COUGH REMEDY
4tbsp cod liver oil
4tbsp clear honey
1tbsp glycerine
the juice of 2 lemons
Shake all the ingredients together in a bottle.
Take a teaspoonful 3 times a day in a
little hot water.

TOM'S BREAKFAST HAM CRUNCHIES

'Can you believe it? Tom tops all this with a fried egg! P'raps we'll give the recipe to Fat Paul,' jokes Brenda.

7oz (250g) lean ham, chopped
7oz (250g) potatoes, grated
1 medium sized onion
1oz (25g) plain flour
1 medium size egg, beaten
1tsp Worcestershire Sauce
pepper and salt
vegetable oil for shallow frying

Simply combine all of the ingredients with salt and pepper and mix well.

Heat the oil in a frying pan and drop in spoonfuls of the mixture. Fry for about 6 minut on each side, turning once. Drain on crumpled kitchen paper.

'Tea made with an infusion of wild thyme works wonders for hangovers,' Tony says.

Breakfast

ble to show positions in oven when cooking two or more
the same time.
The grid positions for the various dishes are numbered from
oven downwards.

Dishes.	Grid Positions in "Regulo" "New World" Ovens.		Reg Sett	
	Cookers with 8 or 9 runners.	Cookers with 5 or 6 runners.		
		2	6	mins.
Eggs baked (greased tins)	2	4		12-15 mins.
Bacon } in same	4	2	6	
Tomatoes sliced } tin	2	4		
	4		7	15-17 mins.
Eggs, poached		2		
Bacon, folded or rolled	3		7	15-17 mins.
on rashers spread over ooms or sliced s in a greased tin		4 2		
gs served on es	5 3	2	6	8-10 mins.
	2	4		
hod 2, }	5			15-17

STILTON, CELERY AND PEAR SOUP

SERVES 4-6

*This soup is excellent for using the left-over Stilton after Christmas.
'Waste not, want not,' as Brian always proclaims.*

1oz (25g) butter or margarine
1 medium onion, finely chopped
3 celery sticks, finely chopped
1tbsp plain flour
1 wine glass dry white wine
20fl oz (1pt/600ml) chicken stock
10fl oz (½pt/300ml) milk
1 large ripe pear (William or
   Conference), peeled and chopped
salt and pepper
4oz (115g) Stilton cheese

Melt the butter in a saucepan, add the onion and celery and cook gently until soft. Stir in the flour and cook for one minute. Gradually add the wine and stock, and stir until thickened and smooth.

Add the milk, pear and seasoning. Cover and simmer for about 20 minutes.

Crumble in the Stilton and stir until melted. Adjust the seasoning and serve piping hot.

UNCLE WALTER'S
WISDOM
'When the elm leaf's like
a mouse's ear
Then sew yer barley, never fear.'

MY RICH VENISON STEW

To allow the venison to develop its full flavour Brian says it should be hung for 1–2 weeks. The marinade will moisten the meat and give it a wonderful spicy taste. This is so very delicious I can almost forgive the stags for making all that noise during the rutting season.

FOR THE MARINADE

1 small onion, chopped
1 celery stick, chopped
1 carrot, sliced
1 strip orange peel
4tbsp oil
5fl oz (¼pt/150ml) red wine
1tsp powdered cinnamon
1tsp mace
6 whole cloves
3lb (1.5kg) boned leg or shoulder of venison, cut into 1 inch (2.5cm) cubes
2oz (55g) butter
8oz (225g) streaky bacon, chopped
2 medium onions, sliced
4tbsp plain flour
3tbsp rowan jelly
1 bouquet garni
1 bay leaf
salt and black pepper
10fl oz (½pt/300ml) port

Mix all the marinade ingredients together and soak the venison cubes in the mixture overnight.

Drain the venison and pat dry. Strain the marinade and reserve the liquid.

Heat the butter in a large heavy-based saucepan. Fry the bacon and onions in the butter until they are transparent. Remove to an ovenproof casserole.

Sauté the venison over a moderate heat, turning to brown evenly. Remove with a slotted spoon to the casserole.

Sprinkle the flour in the pan and add the remaining marinade, stirring all the time, including the residue from the sides of the pan. Stir in the rowan jelly.

Pour this mixture over the venison in the casserole and add the bouquet garni, bay leaf and seasoning. Add the port, cover the casserole and place in the oven at 350°F/180°C/Gas 4 for 2¼ –2½ hours, or until the meat is tender.

Discard the bay leaf and bouquet garni. Serve with baked potatoes and braised celery or red cabbage.

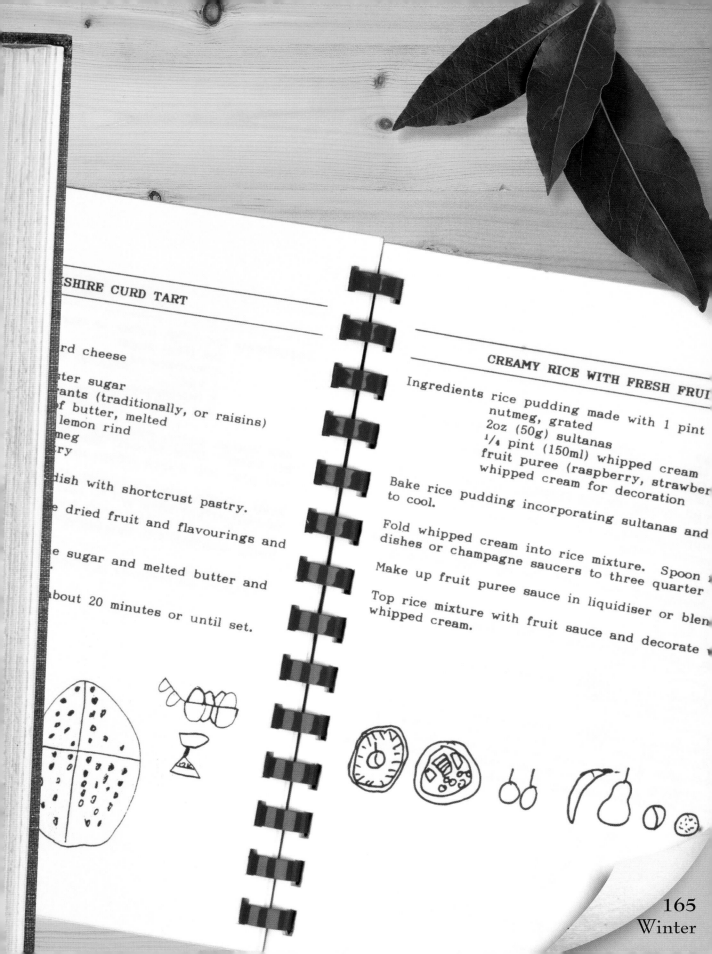

...SHIRE CURD TART

...rd cheese

...ter sugar
...rants (traditionally, or raisins)
...f butter, melted
... lemon rind
...meg
...ry

...dish with shortcrust pastry.

... dried fruit and flavourings and

... sugar and melted butter and

...bout 20 minutes or until set.

CREAMY RICE WITH FRESH FRUI...

Ingredients rice pudding made with 1 pint
nutmeg, grated
2oz (50g) sultanas
1/4 pint (150ml) whipped cream
fruit puree (raspberry, strawber...
whipped cream for decoration

Bake rice pudding incorporating sultanas and ...
to cool.

Fold whipped cream into rice mixture. Spoon ...
dishes or champagne saucers to three quarter...

Make up fruit puree sauce in liquidiser or blen...

Top rice mixture with fruit sauce and decorate ...
whipped cream.

BETTY TUCKER'S BUDGET BAKE

Poor Betty Tucker handed this recipe on to Clarrie, telling her how easy and economical it is. This should be enough for 4 or 5 portions. Her advice was to shrink or stretch the ingredients according to what you find in the larder. When Clarrie makes it, she takes some along to Mike.

1lb (450g) potatoes
2tbsp vegetable oil
½ small firm white cabbage, shredded
8oz (225g) streaky bacon, cut into strips
4oz (115g) mushrooms, sliced
salt and pepper
1 large tin (400g) of chopped tomatoes
1tsp dried herbs
8oz (225g) grated cheddar cheese

Parboil the potatoes, drain and slice.

Heat the oil in a pan and quickly fry the cabbage, bacon and mushrooms until soft, but not brown. Pile into an ovenproof casserole with the sliced potatoes, seasoning and tomatoes. (Make the tomato juice up to 10fl oz (½pt/300ml) with water if necessary.) Sprinkle with herbs and top with grated cheese.

Bake at 350°F/180°C/Gas 4 for 1 hour until browned on top and cooked through.

JOE'S BUBBLE AND SQUEAK

SERVES AT LEAST 2

There is usually a dish of left-over mashed potato in the larder and some remains of the previous day's cooked greens. So when Clarrie's out of the way Joe fries this up with a lump of lard. 'I wish we still had a pot of dripping', he moans.

8oz (225g) cold cabbage or
   brussels sprouts
1lb (450g) mashed potato
1tbsp oil
1 small onion
3 rashers streaky bacon
salt and pepper
3oz (85g) grated cheese

Chop the cabbage and mix with the potato.

Heat the oil in a frying pan, add the chopped onion and the bacon, snipped into thin strips. When the onion is soft, add the potato and cabbage mixture and press down firmly. Season with salt and pepper and fry until the bottom is brown.

Sprinkle the grated cheese on the top and brown under the grill.

NOTES

Creamy mashed potato is made especially good and given a touch of sophistication by sieving the boiled potato and mixing with thick yoghurt and crushed garlic.

APPETIZERS — Tomato Juice, Aspic

SOUPS — Vegetable Stock, Herb Bouquet, Fish Chowders

FISH — Pickled Fish, Crab, Shrimp

EGGS & CHEESE

MEATS — Beef, Veal, Stews, Lamb, Pot Roast, Boiled Ham, Shish Kebab

POULTRY & GAME — Boiled Chicken, Wild Game, Fricassee, Stews

VEGETABLES — Onions, Boiled Potatoes, Green Beans, Carrots, Eggplant, Stewed Tomatoes

SALADS — Fish, Aspic

SAUCES — All Marinades

DESSERTS & BEVERAGES

BAY LEAV...

WALTER GABRIEL'S GINGERNUTS

MAKES ABOUT 24

Granny Perkins used to make these specially for dear old Uncle Walter.
He would dunk them slyly in his tea when he thought she wasn't looking.

4oz (115g) butter or margarine
1tbsp golden syrup
3oz (85g) brown sugar
6oz (175g) self-raising flour
1tsp bicarbonate of soda
1tsp ground ginger
pinch of salt

Put the butter, syrup and sugar together in a pan and melt over a low heat.

Sift together the flour, bicarbonate of soda, ginger and salt, and add these to the melted ingredients in the pan, stirring thoroughly.

Place the mixture in small heaps on a greased baking tray and flatten slightly. Bake for 10–15 minutes at 375°F/190°C/ Gas 5 until golden brown.

MARJORIE'S MARMALADE CAKE

Mrs Antrobus was often seen on her way to the Vicarage to take Robin, who was the vicar then, a freshly baked cake.

6oz (175g) butter
6oz (175g) soft brown sugar
grated zest and juice of
  1 medium orange
3 medium size eggs
2tbsp chunky marmalade
7oz (200g) self-raising flour
1tsp mixed spice
4oz (115g) mixed fruit

Cream together the butter, sugar and orange zest until fluffy. Add the beaten eggs and the marmalade. Fold in the sifted flour and spice. Add the mixed fruit and orange juice and combine thoroughly.

Turn the mixture into a lined and greased 7 in (18cm) cake tin and bake at 350°F/180°C/Gas 4 for 1¼ hours. Leave to cool in the tin before turning.

UNCLE WALTER'S WARMING ORANGE WINE

Boil the zest of 8 large oranges and 4 lemons in 4.5l (8pt) of water. Add the juice of the fruit and 4lb (1.8kg) sugar and stir until dissolved. Sieve and bottle, adding a few large raisins, some bruised ginger root and a clove to each bottle. Leave at room temperature to ferment. Cork.

FARMWORKERS' WARMING WINTER SOUP

A bowl of hearty soup and a chunk of bread is just the thing on a frosty winter's day.

2oz (55g) butter
1½lb (650g) onions, thinly sliced
3 cloves garlic, chopped
2tsp sugar
8oz (225g) potatoes, diced
40fl oz (1.2l/2pt) beef stock
  (or 2 tins consommé)
salt and pepper
½ stick of French bread
2oz (55g) Gruyère cheese, grated

Melt the butter in a saucepan, add the onions, garlic and sugar and cook gently until the onions have browned. Add the potatoes, stock and seasoning. Bring to the boil and simmer for 15–20 minutes.

Slice the bread and toast on one side. Ladle the soup into earthenware bowls and float the pieces of toast on top, toasted side down. Sprinkle the Gruyère cheese on top and place under a hot grill until the cheese bubbles, or bake in a preheated oven at 325°F/160°C/Gas 3.

*'Button yer coat.
Do up yer collar.
Wild geese about.
Bad weather to foller.'*

AUBERGINE, TOMATO AND GREEN LENTIL SALAD

SERVES 6–8

A salad with a difference and, with green lentils still being a fashionable ingredient, it has to be a success! This is darling Debbie's concoction. I wonder if she prepares food like this for Marshall.

4oz (115g) Puy (green) lentils,
  soaked overnight
4 medium aubergines, about 6oz
  (175g) each
4 large tomatoes, skinned and chopped
1 green pepper, deseeded and chopped
1 small onion, chopped

FOR THE DRESSING
6tbsp olive oil
juice of 2 lemons
3 garlic cloves, crushed
3tbsp fresh coriander leaves, chopped
2tsp cumin
½tsp cayenne pepper
1tsp salt

Drain the lentils, cover with fresh water and cook for 30 minutes or until soft. Drain and cool.

Prick the skins of the aubergines and bake at 400°F/200°C/Gas 6 until they are soft and the skins are crinkly. Allow them to cool, then peel. Chop the flesh coarsely into a bowl and add the skinned and chopped tomatoes, lentils, chopped pepper and onion.

To make the dressing, mix the spices and seasoning together with the oil and lemon juice. Add to the aubergines, stirring in some of the coriander, leaving a little to garnish.

INGREDIENTS INDEX

174
Index

CHARACTER INDEX

ACKNOWLEDGEMENTS

I wish to thank Vanessa Whitburn, editor of *The Archers* for giving her support, Kate Oates for her positive and enthusiastic help, and my patient and good-natured editors Jane Trollope and Alison Myer.

I am exceedingly grateful to Sarah Bell for her jolly illustrations, my husband Peter who once again deciphered my scrawl, and Ambridge's inhabitants who welcomed Jennifer into their kitchens, and without whom this book could not have been possible.

PICTURE CREDITS